Rise and Fall of DEVE GOWDA and The Constitutional Breakdown

by
Dr. Janak Raj Jai
M.A., LL.M., J.D., Ph.D. (Law)
Advocate
Supreme Court of India
assisted by
Smt. Santosh Jai

Regency Publications
New Delhi 110 008

The comments and information published in this book are solely of the Author, and the Publisher may or may not agree with them.

ISBN 81-86030-47-6

Published by Regency Publications, 20/36-G, Old Market, West Patel Nagar, New Delhi 110 008 and Printed at Radiant Printers, New Delhi 110 008, Telefax: 578 3571.

Dedicated to the
people of
our country

Preface

The book on Deve Gowda is a supplement to the earlier work, *Commissions and Omissions by Indian Prime Ministers* and *Narasimha Rao—The Best Prime Minister?*

The book contains the chequered history of events that led to Deve Gowda's compromise elevation as India's Twelfth Prime Minister with no mandate.

He is the first Prime Minister who can not read, write or speak the *Rashtra Bhasha*. He is the first whose name came on surface only after the elections were over. He is the first who did not resign the MLA seat after swearing in as a Prime Minister. He is the first who had to seek the support of the 13 parties of different ideologies. He is the first against whom maximum number of Writ Petitions were filed challenging his very appointment as the Prime Minister (not being elected as Member of Parliament). He is the first who embarrassed the Chief Justice of India on account of his late night mysterious meet at the latter's residence. Last but not the least he will be the first who would surely be shown the door by those, who made him adorn this coveted office, for a *quid pro quo*.

The book also highlights the working of the Government consisting of Council of Ministers with different loyalties and ideologies. Unnecessary interference with the working of the judiciary is an unprecedented achievement of this Government. This has been brought out in the book, with the help of expert comments by Jurists and public spirited persons.

The President's role in the formation of the Government supported by 13 political parties as also the active role played by the judiciary in entertaining Public Interest Litigation during these turbulant months, are discussed in the present work.

I earnestly feel indebted to all those, whose comments, opinions, articles etc. have been used to make this work complete in all respects. A few judgements of the High Court of Delhi and the Supreme Court of India also form part of this book to place the matter in proper perspective.

1.3.1997
Sewa Sadan
Rajpur Khurd (near Chhatarpur)
New Delhi 110 068
Ph: 6803447
6932057

Dr. Janak Raj Jai
Advocate
Supreme Court of India

P.S. While the book was being written, we never thought that the UF Government would ever fall before its publication. Since its dramatic and unexpected fall on 11.4.1997, we have added one chapter — *The Dramatic Fall and the Constitutional Breakdown* giving briefly the highlights of the fall of the Government and the Constitutional crisis facing the country.

15.4.1997 Author

Contents

Biographical Sketch

A man, by name, H.D. Deve Gowda who suddenly came on the national scene as the Twelfth Prime Minister of this great country on 1st June, 1996 has a very humble back ground. "The dramatic development pitchforked the 63 year old Deve Gowda a hitherto State politician into the nation's highest executive office as the 12th Prime Minister. From the Cambridge educated, liberal leaning Nehru to the simple civil contractor turned politician H.D. Deve Gowda, the country has seen 12 Prime Ministers since independence."

There is no doubt that H.D. Deve Gowda comes from Village 'Hardanahalli' in Halinarasipura Taluk, District Hassan, Karnataka. He inherits three acres of land which is practically a dry piece of land. He also inherits an ancestral house in the native village. The man today at the highest position indeed started his career from scratch.

Education

Deve Gowda in fact does not have extraordinary educational qualification. After having obtained diploma in Civil Engineering, Deve Gowda started his career as a petty contractor.

Political Career

To his good luck Deve Gowda could not make a mark in his vocation as a contractor. Finding himself in a difficult situation in the profession he decided to try his luck in the field of politics, where he rose to the highest position. It was in the year 1962 when he entered the arena of politics. By his skill, dedication and dogged pursuits, he was able to establish himself within three-four years. He had been very ambitious right from the beginning. He successfully contested the Assembly elections and became a Member of the Legislative Assembly. When Dev Raj Urs was the Chief Minister of the State of Karnataka, Deve Gowda had a prominant position in the Assembly. He developed very good relations with the Chief Minister and made his fortune by leaps and bounds.

After Dev Raj Urs laid down his office of the Chief Minister, R. Gundu Rao became the next Chief Minister. Deve Gowda by his skill and tactfulness developed very good relations with him and soon he became the conscience keeper of the new Chief Minister. Deve Gowda thus developed very good relations with both the Chief Ministers and took maximum advantage of the situation and made his prime place in the state leadership. Slowly and steadily Deve Gowda went on climbing the stairs in the field of politics having an eye on the office of Chief Minister.

After Emergency

During Emergency from 1975 to 1977, lakhs of people including prominent leaders like Jayaprakash Narayan, Morarji Desai, Chandra Shekhar, Bhim Sen Sachhar, Atal Behari Vajpayee, Maharani Vijay Raje Scindia, Maharani Gayatri Devi were sent to Jail, without knowing the hows and whys of their arrest. This was the darkest period of Indira Gandhi's regime in independent India..

After the revocation of emergency, General elections were declared throughout the country. During these elections, the congress faced a crushing defeat. Even Indira Gandhi lost the election. People threw the congress stalwarts in the dustbins like sucked lemons.

In the State of Karnataka, Ram Krishna Hegde, General Secretary of Janata Party played a very prominent role during the elections held after emergency. In that state also the Congress party had to bite dust and was virtually routed in the elections. At the centre, for the first time after independence a non-Congress government came into power, with Morarji Desai as the Prime Minister. The elections throughout the country, were fought under the stewardship of ailing statesman — Lok Nayak Jayaprakash Narayan.

In the State of Karnataka, Ram Krishna Hegde was the tallest person and deserved the office of Chief Minister in his own right. Being too ambitious, Deve Gowda had been hob-nobbing for this coveted position but he failed to achieve this position. The Central leadership thus installed Ram Krishna Hegde, as the Chief Minister of State of Karnataka.

Joins Hegde's Government

Having failed to achieve the highest throne of Chief Minister, Deve Gowda managed a berth in the cabinet of Ram Krishna Hegde. In Hegde's Cabinet Deve Gowda got the prized portfolio of Public Works and Irrigation. In the State of Karnataka, this portfolio was considered to be a gold mine, if one had a wish to mint money and build an empire rightly or wrongly. Shortly after Deve Gowda had taken over as the Public Works and Irrigation Minister, fingers were raised on his style of functioning. When the criticism on the style of his functioning came on the streets, Deve Gowda was left with no other alternative, than to resign from this high position, which he earned after a long struggle in the field of politics.

During his tenure as Public Works and Irrigation Minister, we learn that Deve Gowda built a big cinema hall at Halinarasipura. In due course he became unpopular and ultimately his relations with the Chief Minister Mr. Hegde became strained. When the relations between the Chief Minister and Deve Gowda could not improve there was no other alternative for Deve Gowda but to resign from the cabinet. Immediately after stepping down Deve Gowda started abusing Hegde openly by calling him bigoted brahmin, anti farmer etc. But the generous Hegde did not take him seriously and allowed him to ventilate his outbursts in public.

After the resignation of Ram Krishna Hegde as the Chief Minister, S.R. Bommai was installed as the next successor. Unfortunately the term of Shri S.R. Bommai as the Chief Minister was short-lived as the Janata Party Legislators withdrew their support. There was thus a spell of President's Rule after which elections were held. In those elections held in the year 1989, the Congress party got the majority winning 180 seats out of 225 seats. Deve Gowda contested from two constituencies and he lost the election from both the constituencies. This was a great set back to Deve Gowda's political career. For about two years he remained in wilderness until he was elected for the Lok Sabha in June, 1991 from Hassan constituency on the Samajwadi Janata Party ticket.

Joins Janta Dal

In the year 1993 Deve Gowda joined Janata Dal under the leadership of Ram Krishna Hegde. Forgetting the past misbehaviour of Deve Gowda, Hegde made him the President of Janata Dal and brought him to lime light once again. In the ensuing elections to be held in 1994 both of them worked very hard and were able to secure majority to form the Government. Unfortunately the honey-moon between both of them could not last long as both of them were aspiring for leadership. On the crucial day, 11/12/1994, when the leader of the party was to be elected ugly scenes were seen on the streets which brought shame to the Indian Polity. "On the fateful day, 11-12-1994, Mr. Gowda got his two sons to congregate 5000 bad elements with instructions to beat up Mr. Hegde and his supporters in the premises of the Vidhan Soudha. Some of Hegde's supporters were beaten up, some were disrobed, and bombs were ready to be thrown at the supporters of Hegde but that did not happen. An amazonian lady activist rushed to Mr. Hedge on the pretext of touching his feet and beat him with slippers. There was Pandemonium. People began to run helter skelter for safety. The violent mob gate crashed to Vidhan Soudha, broke the doors and window panes and glasses. A chivalrous youth climbed the tower, removed the flying national tricolour flag and in its place hoisted the Janata Dal Flag. Shri P. Kodandarmaiah who was the police chief on duty and his policemen remained inactive spectators to the ongoing tragic drama that was enacted by the bumper mob under the directions of Mr. Gowda's sons who were there on the spot directing the operations."

Therefore it is clear that in order to become the Chief Minister of Karnataka Deve Gowda chose the path of violence. Because of the unhealthy, undemocratic and ugly situation created by Deve Gowda the Janata Dal Legislature Party was left with no other alternative than to elect Deve Gowda as their leader. Being the Leader of the party Deve Gowda was thus sworn in as the Chief Minister of Karnataka. After becoming the Chief Minister, Deve Gowda tactically continued to administer the Government speaking good words for Hegde for the qualities of his leadership, administrative acumen and seeking his advice in the governance of the state. This was a calculated move of Deve Gowda to neutralize Hegde, the strongman of Karnataka.

To get rid of Hegde from the state scene where he was very popular, Deve Gowda persuaded Hegde to become a Member of Rajya Sabha. Deve Gowda thus succeeded in his plan and sent Hegde in the Upper House as a Member of Rajya Sabha.

Deve Gowda's chequered biographical sketch, therefore, shows that he is a man who has no respect for value based politics, he has no scruples and morals worth mentioning, he is selfish and self centered to the core, he does not see beyond his nose, he is aggressive before the meek and hapless and humble before the strong.

Before he was installed as the 12th Prime Minister of this great country Shri H.D. Deve Gowda had been holding the office of Chief Minister in the State of Karnataka. The way he got this highest position is nothing but just a miracle. And it is only in India that such miracles take place. Even after becoming the Prime Minister, he did not resign his seat of MLA, till he was elected to the Rajya Sabha. Unfortunately, in the by-election from that constituency, his own stooge has been defeated. He is the Prime Minister against whom maximum number of writ petitions have been filed challenging his appointment as Prime Minister. He is also the first Prime Minister who is not able to read, write or speak Rashtra Bhasha — 'Hindi'. He spent a huge sum from public exchequer to be able to address the nation in tooti-phooti Hindi on 15th August 1996, at the Red Fort.

As Prime Minister (1st June, 1996)

During in the 11th Lok Sabha Elections in the country in 1996, no political party was given a clear mandate to form the government. This is not the first time when such a situation arose. But in these elections, the Bhartiya Janata Party came out as the single largest party for the first time in the history of Independent India. The congress party was the second largest party. And the third front (which came into existence after the elections) comprising 13 parties belonging to different ideologies got the third position. All the so called secular parties came together to see that the Bhartiya Janata Party, being a communal party does not form the government at the centre. And every effort, fair or foul, was made to create an anti BJP stance. To refresh the memory of the learned readers it is pertinent to point out that this very party (BJP) successfully shared power when in year 1977 (after emergency) the Janata Party formed the Government at the centre under the leadership of Lok Nayak Jayaprakash Narayan, when Morarji Desai was installed as the Prime Minister of India. Not only this when Vishwa Nath Pratap Singh became the Prime Minister, the same BJP's support was accepted from outside.

Unfortunately a very unhealthy and undemocratic stand had been taken by 13 parties forming a United Front, against the Bhartiya Janata Party. Happily the President of Indian Republic, Dr. Shankar Dayal Sharma, invited Atal Bihari Vajpayee, the leader of Bhartiya Janata Party to form the Government and show his strength on the floor of the House within two weeks. It is a matter of great shame that the United Front criticized, in objectionable language, the role of the President in inviting the largest single party to form the Government. Atal Bihari Vajpayee, when could not prove his majority on the floor of the house, gracefully, as a matured and a seasoned statesman bowed out of the office and tendered resignation of his Government. So the Government headed by BJP under the leadership of Atal Bihari Vajpayee came to an end within 13 days of its installation.

Immediately after the fall of BJP Government a frantic search had been started to find out an acceptable leader to adorn the throne of the Prime Minister. To start with, the United Front considered the names of Jyoti Basu, V.P. Singh, Ram Krishna Hegde and Laloo Prasad Yadav. First of all Jyoti Basu and Laloo Prasad were contacted but both of them expressed their inability to shift to the centre. Raja Vishwanath Pratap Singh played hide and seek game and made himself unavailable to the callers. After the disinclination of these three leaders, the chances of Ram Krishna Hegde were almost certain to head the government at the centre. But the leaders of the Janata Dal including Laloo Prasad Yadav were not in favour of installing Hegde as the Prime Minister. It is unfortunate that the so-called secular anti brahmin lobby opposed the name of Hedge on caste lines. Does this at all behove the so-called secularists to consider the name for this august office on caste basis?

Ultimately, H.D. Deve Gowda, the Chief Minister of Karnataka, became the choice of all the ghataks of the United Front to adorn the chair of the Prime Minister, which was adorned in the first instance by Jawaharlal Nehru for seventeen years from 1947 to 1964. The choice of Deve Gowda, therefore, was not on merits but was a selection of a name by the leader purely on caste lines, and expediency. The top most-leader of Karnataka, Ram Krishna Hegde, of course, had the guts to speak his mind and openly characterised the selection of Deve Gowda as one not based on consensus and concurrence of all the leaders of the party. He further called the hotch-potch alliance "opportunistic" and unprincipled.

Takes Oath as a Prime Minister

Deve Gowda took an oath as Prime Minister on 1st June 1996. Although he had resigned from the office of Chief Minister, yet he had not vacated the seat of MLA from the Karnataka Legislative Assembly. While administering him an oath of office of Prime Minister the President gave Deve Gowda time till 12th June, 1996 to prove his majority on the floor of the House. After winning the vote of confidence in the House on 12th June, 1996 the first item on his agenda was the expulsion of Shri Ram Krishna Hegde (who had earlier been his Patron Saint) from the party. Such was the venom and vendatta Deve Gowda carried against Hegde.

Hegde Sacked

After he won the vote of confidence, Deve Gowda went to the house of each and every leader and successfully convinced everyone for the sack of Hegde. The result was that within 24 hours of winning the vote of confidence, Deve Gowda was able to announce the expulsion of Ram Krishna Hegde from the party. Though there was reluctance from certain quarters on this harsh decision, but Deve Gowda had his say being the newly appointed Prime Minister.

Bad Omen: The day, Deve Gowda took oath of office of the Prime Minister i.e. 1st June, 1996 the chief of the Delhi Unit of Janata Dal resigned with most of the office bearers one day before the oath taking ceremony.

Speaking to the *Times of India*, Viresh Pratap Choudhry said "I have taken the most important decision of my life." Choudhry attributed his resignation to the Janata Dal forming the Government with the support of Congress, which he said "is identified with perversion of value based politics, with the emergency. . . ." Choudhry further claimed that he was leaving the party along with two thirds of the office bearers and six out of the Eleven Presidents of the party's district cells as "My colleagues and I are unable to countenance this volte face by the Janata Dal."

Maneka Gandhi Expelled

Meneka Gandhi was another prominent Janata Dal leader and a Member of Parliament from Pilibheet who launched a tirade on Deve Gowda for the manner of constituting the cabinet and underlined the powerlessness of the Prime Minister, Deve Gowda. She is on record to say that "several of his Ministers were ninecompoops. The only qualification of the ministers was singing songs in praise of their mentor Mr. Laloo Prasad Yadav which was enough to secure berths in the Council of Ministers which was "an exercise in compromise". For calling a spade a spade, Maneka Gandhi paid a very heavy price and even had to face expulsion from the party.

President Faltered

By inviting Deve Gowda, who was neither a member of the Lok Sabha nor had any following nor experience or maturity to hold this most enviable position, the President came under criticism from certain quarters. If the President had gone through the earlier decision of his predecessor, he would not have ventured to repeat the same mistake. Shri R. Venkataraman, the then President of India had a bitter experience of such type of minority government when Chandra Shekhar was the Prime Minister with the support of the Congress party headed by late Shri Rajiv Gandhi. Inspite of assurance by Rajiv Gandhi that his party would extend support for one year, Chandra Shekhar had to lay down his office as the Prime Minister of India because Rajiv Gandhi threatened to withdraw the support. To quote from the book "My Presidential Years" by R. Venkataraman (pp. 482).

> "I did not accept the resignation without feeling sorry for Chandra Shekhar. During his few months in office he handled Parliament competently and was responsive to suggestions from the opposition. He was under constant strain from the pressures of the Congress party, which I am afraid assumed that it was the real government and Chandra Shekhar only a proxy. The Office hungry coterie of the Congress party used to misguide Rajiv Gandhi that Chandra Shekhar's attempts at building up a good image could prove deleterious to his image. Looking back after two years, I realise my naiveness in accepting the Congress assurance of "unconditional support" to Chandra Shekhar. I had expected the support to last a year atleast. I realised that unequal combinations are always disadvantageous to the weaker side."

Hegde's Frank Expression on the Unholy Alliance, at "Meet the Press" Programme

Senior Janata Dal leader Ramkrishna Hegde, on Monday virtually questioned the post-poll cobbling up of Third Front and its coalition arrangement with Congress, fearing that it might be considered an "opportunistic alliance to grab power".

Mr Hegde, who was once projected as a Prime Ministerial candidate, and had mooted a pre-election coalition arrangement with the Congress only to be rebuffed by his own partymen, said the alliance should have been forged in the pre-election scene to inspire people's confidence.

"We will not be able to carry conviction with the people that we are not coming together to grab power but are doing so in the interest of the country," the former Chief Minister told a meet-the-press programme organised by the Bangalore Reporters' Guild here.

Meanwhile, the 14-party Third Front has formally named as the United Front, following a decision of the Steering Committee that met in New Delhi.

With the decision to give a formal name to the political group, hitherto referred to as the Third Front, the multi-party alliance has become a definite entity that will enter the 11th Lok Sabha as the United Front.

Mr Hegde also took potshots at Janata Dal leaders, targeting former Prime Minister V.P. Singh, who had pooh-poohed the coalition with the Congress he had mooted before the elections and had even accused him of trying to join the Congress.

He was also unsparing in his denouncement of the "unbecoming conduct" of some Third Front leaders when they met President Shankar Dayal Sharma to protest his decision to invite BJP to form the government and stayed away from a protest dharna held here by the Third Front against presidential decision.

"I will not participate in it. I don't find any reason to protest (against the President)," a visibly agitated Mr Hegde said, as he chastised some Third Front leaders who had reportedly made intemperate remarks against Dr. Sharma during their meeting with the President.

Mr Hegde said it was unbecoming of "some of my friends" to have attacked Dr. Sharma, who had an unblemished record, and was only following "exactly the chapter and words (in the Constitution)."

Mr Hegde recalled that he had repeatedly been stressing even before the elections that an alliance forged after the polls would be construed as opportunistic by the people and hence it should precede the polls on the basis of a national agenda.

He said cobbling up of a coalition after the elections could not be called a mandate and added that "if one talks in terms of mandate, there are three mandates, for NF-LF combine, for the Congress and for the BJP."

"If 17 parties claim we have the mandate, what is its meaning," Mr Hegde asked and pointed that "We (some are in the Third Front) had fought against each other. If we join together, can we say it is a mandate. Mandate has sanctity."

Significantly, Mr Hegde also referred to a question raised by another Janata Dal stalwart Biju Patnaik who had reportedly wondered how four chief ministers could decide who should be the Prime Minister, apparently referring to the selection of Third Front's Prime Ministerial candidate.

Mr Hegde, however, backed the candidature of Mr Deve Gowda as the Third Front's leader and said he had never nursed the ambition or "illusion" of becoming the Prime Minister.

Complimenting Mr Gowda for providing "good leadership" at the State-level, Mr Hegde said he was capable of repeating the same at the national level also. "If only I was invited for the meeting, I would have been the happiest person to propose Mr Gowda's name (for the Prime Minister's post)," he said.

Mr Hegde cited the case of BJP forging an alliance with the Shiv Sena, Haryana Vikas Party, Samata Party and the Akali Dal before the polls and said, "It does not create any confusion."

Mr Hegde also released a letter he had written to some eminent people in November last visualising that no party would secure majority, that BJP might emerge as the single-largest party and that a coalition of secular forces should be formed on the basis of a national agenda.

He wondered who could assure that post-poll coalition arrangement would be stable and recalled that in 1979, Mr Charan Singh could not face Parliament even for a single day after he parted company with the then Janata Party and formed the Government with Congress' support and also that Mr Chandra Shekhar also "fell into Rajiv Gandhi's trap and his Government collapsed."

Asked if the Third Front should support formation of a Congress Government headed by Mr P.V. Narasimha Rao in the event of the BJP Ministry's collapse, he said, "The Third Front has to decide the issue."

He noted that the Congress had secured 30 per cent of the votes and that it also had undergone changes. "The party's 'I' appellation has also gone," he said. Mr Hegde said if the Vajpayee's Ministry fell, it was for the President to decide whether to invite the Congress or the Third Front to form the government. "If a situation arises wherein no one is able to run the Government, then obviously we have to seek a fresh mandate."

Pioneer News Service adds: Janata Dal spokesperson S. Jaipal Reddy refused to react to the statement of Mr Hegde expressing reservations on the formation of a Third Front Government. Mr Reddy said he was not aware of any such statement and, therefore, could not react to it.

Senior Dal leaders, however, were not surprised over Mr Hegde's reaction. They felt he had been nursing a grouse against his colleague, Mr Gowda, who had been selected the Front's leader for the prime ministership.

In New Delhi, the Steering Committee's meeting for renaming of the Third Front as the United Front was attended by leaders of the Janata Dal, Left parties, Samajwadi Party, Tamil Manila Congress (TMC), All India Indira Congress, Madhya Pradesh Vikas Congress and the Telugu Desam at Andhra Bhawan.

Among those who attended the meeting were Mr Ram Vilas Paswan, Mr Sharad Yadav and Mr Jaipal Reddy from the Janata Dal, Mr Ial Jan Pasha from the TDP, Mr Mulayam Singh Yadav from the Samajwadi Party, Mr Arjun Singh from the Indira Congress, Mr P. Chidambaram from the TMC and Mr Madhavrao Scindia from MPVC. The Left parties were represented by Mr Harkishan Singh Surjeet and Mr Sitaram Yechuri from CPI (M), Mr Indrajit Gupta and Mr D. Raja from CPI and Mr Abani Roy from the Revolutionary Socialist Party.

The Congress is not part of the front and will support it from outside, Left leaders said. The birth of the United Front was announced at a public meeting on Monday evening at V.P. House where one leader from each of the parties in the Front spoke.

Meanwhile, Front spokesperson Jaipal Reddy denied that any preconditions were laid down by the Congress in extending support to it.

Courtesy: *Pioneer,* 21.5.1996

Maneka Gandhi also speaks out her mind

"Deve Gowda offered me three ministries"

Maneka Gandhi, India's self-styled environmental apostle, came back from political oblivion to contest the 1996 general election. With the government desperately looking for women to be made ministers, her name did the rounds in the rumour stage. But expansion after expansion, her name was missing from the list of ministers. And suddenly, Maneka came back to the front pages with statements criticising the government on the Cogentrix deal. Ritu Sarin spoke to her at length hours before she was expelled from the J.D. Excerpts:

❑ **Why did you raise the issue of the Cogentrix deal at this point? Former Power Secretary, R. Vasudevan, has said some expert committees did clear the project when the Congress was in power.**

Nobody cleared it. The Centre at one point had marked out 100 objections to the project but none of the objections were met and in January, 1996 they signed the power purchase agreement with Cogentrix. There were three environmental committees which went to Karnataka but did not clear it. Vasudevan was the power secretary who gave a conditional clearance but it was a power clearence. In India, you cannot go ahead with such a project till you get an environmental clearance.

The fact of the matter is that everything was hanging fire till Deve Gowda became Prime Minister. The moment he became Prime Minister on June 2, he sent for the file as a first case and the next day cleared it. I would say the same person has broken every law back in the state. He has got no pollution clearance from Karnataka, he has made the Secretary, Environment in the state resign on the issue, the Karnataka Environment committee has rejected it, there are thousands of people protesting against it, and in spite of that he cleared it. This is all suspicious.

❑ **What are the ramifications of the Cogentrix deal?**

This is a scandal of the proportion of Bofors. Now, the attempt is to give out complete lies. Gowda did not even let the Environment Ministry look at the files. The Environment Minister, J.N. Nishad, has said the case had been cleared but he did not see the files till two days ago, after I had raised the issue.

❑ **The Bofors controversy centred on the recepients of the kickbacks in the gun deal. Who do you think took the kickbacks in the Cogentrix deal?**

Someone who was in such a hurry to pass it, obviously. I can only say that the needle of suspicion points to anyone who is over-eager to pass something without any rule of law.

❑ **In this case, who is it?**

If the needle of suspicion points to the Prime Minister, then he must clear his name. Now, they are trying to trivialise the issue because they are so frightened. They are saying I am raising this issue because I was not made a minister, because I am close to Hegde and the BJP and because I wanted to become the Lt. Governor.

❑ **Did you really ask Gowda for a berth in the Cabinet?**

In this Government, there is a Cabinet expansion every week. There is no question of not becoming a minister if I wanted. I won my seat by the largest majority in India. I am the only JD MP from UP and the state Assembly elections are due shortly. If I wanted a berth, I would have got one. I have been asked by the Prime Minister three times on what I would like to be and I have replied each time, nothing.

❑ **Wouldn't you have liked to be the Environment Minister again? Were you offered the portfolio?**

I never asked for anything. But he offered me more than one ministry and you can check this up with Jyoti Basu and Narasimha Rao who were consulted on what I should get. They all suggested different portfolios for me. They ranged from Culture, Environment to I&B. I said no to all. People are talking about the timing of raking up the Cogentrix issue, but the moment I got to know about it, I even told the Prime Minister I was going to raise it. When I telephoned him he said, 'Amma give me four days, amma give me four days. I will make you minister'. This was after the second expansion. I finally told him I would not even give you four minutes because I figured he did not understand what I was talking about.

❑ **Laloo Prasad Yadav has said you asked to be appointed Lt. Governor. Is this true?**

No. I would like to be the LG, but it is not true that I asked them for it.

❑ **In your letter to the Prime Minister you have asked for probity in public life and asked for an enquiry into the assets of all cabinet ministers. What are you implying by this?**

See, one man is raided and you find he has Rs 9 crore in his house. The next day you make him a minister. Then you take a man who is wanted for rape and you put him in as Minister of State for Home. You have allegations in the Jain Hawala case pending against Bommai and Sharad Yadav who becomes the party's working president. At the same time you keep out ND Tewari and Madhav Rao Scindia using the excuse of the Jain Hawala case.

So, are we going to attack people who are asking for a probe on dishonesty and corruption or are you going to attack the dishonest and corrupt?

❑ **The party president, Laloo Prasad Yadav has made some serious personal allegations against you.**

Laloo Prasad Yadav has got the largest scandal ever known in India attached to him. You have misused funds which have gone into thousands of crores and have bankrupted a state like Bihar. Could all this have happened without him? Who can make money in Bihar without siphoning it right to the top? So, you have a president who faces corruption charges, you have a working president under corruption charges, you have a prime minister against whom I am making allegations saying there was unseeming haste in clearing the project which leads to suspicion of corruption. What type of party are we running?

❑ **What do you think of the manner in which Gowda handled other environmentally-sensitive issues like the entry of the KFC and Pizza Hut and even the Tehri issue?**

Let us look at the KFC issue. They have broken every law to come in. Every technical committee rejected it and I see a clear pattern in which the real issue has been obfuscated here and in the Cogentrix case.

Even in the case of Tehri, I was one of the first person to rake up the issue as minister. This time, (Sundarlal) Bahuguna asked me to intervene and I said no, Gowda has done this to me before.

Let me give you the background. The present prime minister as chief minister met me, VP Singh, Chandra Shekhar and Dig Vijay Singh and he assured us he would not give KFC the licence. Two days later he gave it. Not only that, officials of KFC said they were made to pay because Maneka Gandhi was in the picture. Their rates went up. After it began, Gowda himself asked me to come to Bangalore to make a fuss about it, and all it did was that the rates were upped again.

Then, we held a seminar and Gowda said, 'get a sample' and we got a sample which contained msg. We went to him and he said "No problem", and again the rates went up. So, when Bahuguna asked me to bring him to Tehri, I said no because, all I was going to do was to put money in his pocket again.

Every action of his is linked to a pattern of events where he gets environmentalists involved, we raise our voices, the contractors move in.

Courtesy: *Indian Express,* 7.7.1996

Council of Ministers & Portfolios

Prime Minister

H. D. Deve Gowda

Prime Minister and also in charge of the Ministries/Departments of Agriculture, Home Affairs, Science and Technology, Personnel, Public Grievances and Pensions, Atomic Energy, and the other Ministries/Departments not allocated to any other Cabinet Minister, viz. Chemicals and Fertilisers, Communications, Environment and Forests, Food Processing Industries, Health and Family Welfare, Mines, Non-Conventional Energy

Sources, Petroleum and Natural Gas, Planning and Programme Implementation, Power, Steel, Textiles, Electronics, Jammu & Kashmir Affairs, Ocean Development and Space.

Cabinet Ministers

Sh. Balwant S. Ramoowalia	Minister of Welfare and additional charge of the office of the Minister of Labour.
Sh. Birendra Pr. Baishya	Minister of Steel and Minister of Mines.
Sh. C.M. Ibrahim	Minister of Civil Aviation, with additional charge of the Ministry of Information and Broadcasting.
Sh. Chaturanan Mishra	Minister of Agriculture, excluding the Department of Animal Husbandry and Dairying.
Sh. Devendra Prasad Yadav	Minister of Food and Minister of Civil Supplies, Consumer Affairs and Public Distribution.
Sh. I.K. Gujral	Minister of External Affairs
Sh. Indrajit Gupta	Minister of Home Affairs
Sh. Janeshwar Mishra	Minister of Water Resources
Sh. M. Arunachalam	Minister of Labour
Sh. Mulayam Singh Yadav	Minister of Defence
Sh. Murasoli Maran	Minister of Industry
Sh. P. Chidambaram	Minister of Finance and Minister of Department of Company Affairs.
Sh. Ram Vilas Paswan	Minister of Railways.
Sh. S.R. Bommai	Minister of Human Resource Development.
Sh. Srikanta Kumar Jena	Minister of Parliamentary Affairs and Minister of Tourism.
Sh. T.G. Venkatraman	Minister of Surface Transport.
Sh. Yerran Naidu	Minister of Rural Areas and Employment.

Sh. R.L. Jalappa	Minister of Textiles.
Sh. Beni Prasad Varma	Minister of Communications.

Minister of State (Independent Charge)

Sh. Bolla Buli Ramaiah	Minister of State (independent charge) of the Ministry of Commerce.
Sh. Dilip Kumar Ray	Minister of State (Independent charge) of the Department of Animal Husbandry and Dairying in the Ministry of Agriculture.
Capt. Jai Narayan Prasad Nishad	Minister of State (Independent charge) of the Ministry of Environment and Forests.
Smt. Kanti Singh	Minister of State (Independent charge) of the Ministry of Coal.
Sh. Ramakant D. Khalap	Minister of State (Independent charge) of the Departments of Law and Justice.
Dr. S. Venugopalchari	Minister of State in the Ministry of Power and Minister of State in the Ministry of Non-Conventional Energy Sources.
Dr. S. Venkateswarlu	Minister of State in the Ministry of Urban Affairs and Employment and Minister of State in the Ministry of Parliamentary Affairs.
Sh. Saleem Iqbal Shervani	Minister of State (Independent charge) of the Ministry of Health and Family Welfare.
Sh. Shees Ram Ola	Minister of State (Independent charge) of the Ministry of Chemicals and Fertilizers.
Sh. Yogendra K. Alagh	Minister of State (Independent charge) of the Ministry of Planning and Programme Implementation and Minister of

State (Independent charge) of the Ministry of Science and Technology.

Minister of State

Sh. Balasubramanian S.R.	Minister of State in the Ministry of Personnel, Public Grievances and Pensions and Minister of State in the Ministry of Parliamentary Affairs.
Sh. Chandradeo P. Varma	Minister of State in the Ministry of Rural Areas and Employment.
Sh. Dhanushkodi Athithan R.	Minister of State in the Department of Youth Affairs and Sports in the Ministry of Human Resource Development.
Sh. Maqbool Dar	Minister of State in the Ministry of Home Affairs.
Sh. Muhi Ram Saikia	Minister of State in the Department of Education in the Ministry of Human Resource Development.
Sh. N.V.N. Somu	Minister of State in the Ministry of Defence
Sh. T.R. Balu	Minister of State in the Ministry of Petroleum and Natural Gas.

The United Front — A Common Approach to Major Policy Matters and A Minimum Programme

The Background

The United Front has been formed at a crucial moment in our nation's history. The 1996 Lok Sabha elections have given a decisive mandate in favour of secular and democratic forces. Three out of four voters have voted against sectarian and communal parties. At the same time we recognise that these three out of four voters have voted for a number of parties including national and state-level parties. These voters have also voted for a government which is guided by the principles of probity, responsibility with accountability and openness and transparency in all decision-making. We, therefore, interpret the verdict as a mandate for the formation of a secular, liberal and democratic coalition government at the Centre. It is only such a Government that can reflect the pluralistic nature of our society.

The United Front represents the diversity of India in substantial measure. We pledge to represent the resolve of the Indian people to preserve the secular nature of their heritage. We pledge to represent the resolve of the Indian people to give themselves a Government that is representative, responsible and responsive. We pledge to represent the will of the Indian people to strengthen the forces of political federalism which in the Indian context means a strong Centre, strong States and viable local bodies. We pledge to represent the desire of the Indian people to give themselves a higher standard of living and a better quality of life through faster economic growth and enhanced social justice.

The United Front government will not be a replacement of one set of rulers by another. It will mark the beginning of an alternative model of governance based on federalism, decentralisation, accountability, equality and social justice, economic and political reforms, respect for human freedoms and openness and transparency which will ensure the dignity of both the nation and the individual citizen.

The United Front presents below an agenda for a Central government founded on the pillars of unity, secularism, stability, development and distributive justice.

Stability and Federalism

The United Front is committed to giving a stable government at the Centre for the full term of five years. In any coalition, there will be differences, but what is important is the manner in which these differences are aired, discussed and resolved. During its term of office, the United Front government will advance the principles of political, administrative and economic federalism. In each of these spheres powers will be devolved and authority will be decentralised. The last review of Centre-State relations was undertaken by the Sarkaria Commission which gave its report over ten years ago. Since then, there has been a sea-change in both the politics and economics of the country. There has also been a new articulation of States' rights and the need for greater powers to the States to meet the aspirations of their respective States.

Hence, the United Front government intends to pursue a two track policy: On the first track, the recommendations of the Sarkaria Commission on which there is already a broad consensus will be implemented through legislation and administrative action as appropriate. The United Front believes that it is possible to take immediate action, legislative and/or administrative, on the following matters:

(i) to give greater autonomy to States in determining their priorities in developmental programmes;
(ii) to give States greater freedom to draw their State plans within the broad framework of the National Five Year Plans;

(iii) to transfer most centrally sponsored schemes to the control of the State Governments;

(iv) to grant assent promptly to Bills passed by State Legislatures on matters which are within the legislative powers of the State Legislatures.

On the second track, the United Front government will immediately appoint a High-Level Committee to review and update the recommendations of the Sarkaria Commission. The Committee will be requested to also look into the vital question of devolution of financial powers from the Central government to the State governments. The Committee will be required to give its report within three months. The report of the Committee will then be made public so that there is an informed public debate before final decisions are taken.

Besides, the United Front government will reactivate and energise institutions like the National Development Council and the Inter State Council.

The scope of Article 356 of the Constitution has been interpreted and circumscribed by recent decisions of the Supreme Court. Article 356 will be amended to reflect these decisions and to prevent the misuse of that Article.

Elections have been held in most States to Panchayats and, in some cases, also to the Nagarpalikas pursuant to the 72nd and 73rd Amendments, administrative and financial powers to Panchayats and Nagarpalikas in all the States. Steps will be taken to ensure that regular elections are held according to the prescribed frequency.

Social Justice

The United Front is committed to the empowerment of the underprivileged and deprived sections and communities. One-third of the elected membership in Parliament and State Legislatures will be reserved for women. Legislation, including an amendment to the Constitution, if necessary, will be introduced to reserve one-third of all posts in Government for women. The United Front government will take all possible measures to promote and ensure gender equality. All laws will be reviewed to remove provisions which discriminate against women.

The policy of reservation in public employment for Scheduled Castes, Scheduled Tribes and Other Backward Classes will continue and will be implemented vigorously. The benefits of reservation will be extended to dalit Christians. Special courts will be set up under the Scheduled Castes and Scheduled Tribes (Prevention of Atrocities) Act to ensure quick justice to victims of atrocities.

Artisans, craftspersons, tradespersons, weavers and fishermen are among the most neglected sections of society. Special programmes will be devised to enhance their skills, give them modern tools and more credit facilities and make their products and services more marketable so that they will earn living wages.

The United Front government will urge the State governments to take up, on a priority basis, the question of conferring ownership rights on slum dwellers in respect of the land on which they live with suitable provisions for slum improvement, public or private group housing to replace kutcha shelters and allotment of alternative sites in case it becomes necessary to relocate slum dwellers on grounds of public interest.

Empowerment of Scheduled Tribes, Scheduled Castes and Other Backward Classes

Scheduled Tribes are found in many parts of India and dwell in the most difficult and inhospitable terrains. There is growing disaffection among Scheduled Tribes because of lack of security, alienation of their lands, exploitation of the mineral wealth, deprivation of their rights to forest produce and wealth and despoiling of their environment. The United Front Government will appoint a High Level Commission to enquire unto and report on the status, problems and aspirations of the members belonging to the Scheduled Tribes. The United Front government will also study the conclusions contained in the report of the Bhuria Committee on Scheduled Tribes made in 1995 and take necessary steps to implement the salient recommendations.

The United Front government will urge the State government to make legislation for conferring ownership rights in respect of minor forest produce, including Tendu Patta on Scheduled Castes, Scheduled Tribes, Other Backward Classes and other weaker sections who work in the forests. The Central government will consider extending some financial assistance to the State governments which take up this responsibility.

A large number of members belonging to the Scheduled Castes and Other Backward Classes are dependent on their traditional occupations. On the one hand the door of access to other occupations has been barred to them while, on the other hand, there is a sharp dwindling of opportunities and income in their traditional occupations. Despite the policy of reservation there is no true equality of opportunity. The Central government and the State governments have not addressed themselves comprehensively and consistently to measures which would bring economic freedom, educational equality and true equality of opportunities to these people. The United Front government will carefully study the Dalit Manifesto formulated by the National Action Forum For Social Justice and implement its salient recommendations.

A number of cases are pending consideration for inclusion in the list of Scheduled Tribes. Decisions will be taken on these cases expeditiously.

Secularism

The United Front is founded on the plank of secularism and democracy. The United Front declares that secularism means that there should be separation of State and religion and also notes that it is this definition that has been accepted as correct by the Supreme Court in numerous decisions. Attempts by sectarian or communal forces to erode the multi-ethnic, multi-religious and multi-linguistic character of our society will be strongly resisted.

The contentious issue of Babri Masjid-Ram Janmabhoomi will be referred to the Supreme Court under Article 138(2) of the Constitution. Stringent steps will be taken to implement the Protection of Places of Worship Act.

The Constitutional rights to freedom of religion contained in Articles 25, 26, 27 and 28 of the Constitution will be respected and protected. At the same time, the United Front government will not allow obscurantism and fundamentalism from any source and of any sort. The personal codes of different religious communities will not be altered unless and until a consensus has emerged in the religious community concerned for bringing about a change. Untiring efforts will be made to bring every section of the society together to build a strong, modern, forward-looking, liberal and democratic society imbued with a scientific temper and an aspiration for material progress.

The United Front government will review and, if necessary, enlarge the 15-point programme for the minorities and ensure the implementation of the programme. Special emphasis will be placed on finding solutions to the problems of the minorities in relation to education, employment and opportunities for economic betterment.

Towards a Just and Humane Society

The United Front government will, in close cooperation with State governments, take steps to build a just and humane society. The right to free and compulsory elementary education shall be made a fundamental right and enforced through suitable statutory measures. Special programmes will also be launched to take care of children and the disabled and to eradicate child labour in all occupations and industries.

The Indian Penal Code, the Criminal Procedure Code and all other penal laws will be reviewed and amended to make their provisions consistent with the sanctity of human rights. The United Nations Convention on Torture will be adopted. State governments will be required to appoint Human Rights Commissions.

Economic Policies

Growth with social justice will be the motto of the United Front government. There is no substitute for growth. It is growth which creates jobs and generates incomes. Self-reliance has been an article of faith since Independence and the United Front government will adopt such growth-oriented policies that lead to greater self-reliance. The United Front is committed to faster economic growth. The country's GDP needs to grow at over 7% per year in the next 10 years in order to abolish endemic poverty and unemployment. The Ninth Five Year Plan is scheduled to be launched on 1st April 1997. The United Front government will, within 6 months, bring out a detailed document that will articulate the priorities and programmes of the Ninth Plan.

Agriculture

The Agriculture sector cries out for reforms. No strategy of economic reforms and regeneration in India can succeed without sustained and broadbased agricultural development. The rate of investment in agriculture will be stepped up. All controls and regulations that are in the way of increasing the incomes of farmers will be reviewed immediately and abolished wherever found unnecessary. Controls on the movement of agricultural products and on the processing of agricultural products will be abolished. Measures will be taken to ensure that farmers receive fair and remunerative prices for their produce. Special attention will be devoted to augmenting rural infrastructure. A special plan for infrastructure development will be taken up in the 100 most backward and poorest districts of the country. The rural credit system will be restructured so as to double the flow of credit to agriculture and agro-industries, particularly to small and marginal farmers, within 5 years. A national policy on water sharing and water management will be devised in order to save farmers all over the country from recurrent floods and droughts.

Agencies that supply inputs to farmers will be professionalised and where found feasible converted into farmer-owned cooperatives. Agricultural research and extension organisations will be thoroughly overhauled. The most modern technology will be brought to the farm sector, e.g. bio-technology for livestock and cold storage for agro-processing.

A comprehensive law will be made by Parliament in respect of agricultural workers to guarantee them minimum wages and fair conditions of work, group insurance and other rights.

States will be encouraged to implement land reforms by plugging the legal and administrative loopholes. States will also be urged to make a law dealing with land records including record of tenancy rights. In cooperation with the States, larger funds will be allocated for irrigation and extension of cultivation.

Poverty Alleviation

A frontal attack on poverty is an important element in any development policy. This is the main rationale for anti-poverty programmes. Such programmes must be redesigned to ensure generation of more employment, creation of assets, imparting productive skills and raising the incomes of the very poor so that a significant number is brought above the poverty line every year and poverty, as we have known it, is abolished by the year 2005. The United Front government will review all the anti-poverty programmes with a view to strengthening them and providing them with larger funds. A programme for guaranteeing 100 days of employment for every unemployed person will be implemented through Panchayati Raj institutions.

Industry

The key to faster economic growth is rapid, labour-intensive industrialisation. The United Front is committed to maintain a 12% annual growth in the industrial sector. This will require massive capital and modern technology, apart from continuing the process of deregulation and decontrol as required. There is ample room for public investment as well as private investment. When it is required to face competition, domestic industry will be assured of a level playing field.

Suitable policies will be devised to stimulate domestic savings and capital formation. The bulk of the industry's requirements will indeed come from within the country. However, at the margin, the country cannot do without foreign investment particularly if that foreign investment will also bring modern technology and management practices and create new markets for products manufactured in the country. The nation needs and has the capacity to absorb at least $10 billion a year as foreign direct investment.

Suitable credit and taxation policies will be devised to ensure that the bulk of new investments, both domestic and foreign, will be channelled into the core and infrastructure sectors. Entry of multinational companies into low priority areas will be discouraged through suitable fiscal and other measures. In order to promote even development, suitable incentives and policies will be devised to encourage new Industries to locate in the backward districts of the country.

The United Front recognises the role of the corporate sector in building a strong and modern India. The corporate sector should create conditions in which the working class of the country is able to make its contribution with enthusiasm. The United Front government in its dealings with the corporate sector will follow a policy informed by transparency and fair play and expects that the corporate sector will reciprocate by following the rules and conventions of a healthy market economy. The corporate sector should also keep in mind the paramount interest of the consumer and will be held accountable through an expanded network of consumer courts. The United Front government will always be ready to engage in a meaningful and constructive dialogue with the corporate sector with a view to strengthening the Indian economy.

The progress towards the goal of bringing India's tariffs in accord with world levels will be measured and calibrated. An independent Tariff Commission will be appointed within three months to hear and determine tariff disputes as well as to recommend appropriate levels of tariffs for different products and different industries keeping in view the larger interests of the country.

There are a number of domestic industries which are essentially home-based or village-based requiring low skills and employing a large number of people. These industries will be given adequate protection and it will be ensured that foreign investment does not displace such industries.

The balance among large, medium and small/cottage industries will be restored. Small and cottage industries have the potential of creating large job opportunities. They are also more elastic in responding to changes in the market. Hence, special plans will be devised to promote small and cottage industries to achieve the twin objectives of growth and employment.

Public Sector

In the early decades of development, the public sector played a pioneering role. The public sector will continue to be an important component of Indian industry. The United Front government will help to make the public sector strong and competitive. In a competitive and technology-driven economy, there is no room for monopolies and inefficiency. Public sector enterprises which are essentially commercial enterprises should conduct their business on commercial lines. They should show a healthy return on the capital employed. It is widely acknowledged that the public sector requires to be reformed and restructured. The United Front government will identify public sector companies that have comparative advantages and will support them in their drive to become global giants. Other profit making and efficient public sector companies will be strengthened and their managements professionalised, and participation of workers in the management of these companies will be encouraged. Sick or potentially sick public sector companies will be rehabilitated through a menu of options that may include handing over the management to professional groups or workers' cooperatives.

The question of withdrawing the public sector from non-core and non-strategic areas will be carefully examined subject, however, to assuring the workers and employees of job security or, in the alternative, opportunities for retraining and redeployment. The United Front government will establish a Disinvestment Commission to advise the government on these steps. Any decision to disinvest will be taken and implemented in a transparent manner. Revenues generated from such disinvestment will be utilised in two vital areas, health and education, particularly in the poorer and backward districts of the country. A part of such revenues will be earmarked to create an investment fund which will be used to strengthen other public sector enterprises.

Industrial Sickness

A new law will be made to deal with industrial sickness and the Board for industrial and Financial Reconstruction will be completely revamped. The law will also provide for a separate mechanism to deal with sickness in small industries. Efforts will be made to rehabilitate and revive sick industries and protect the interest of the workers.

Labour

Workers form the backbone of the industrial sector. Their rights are spelt out in a number of laws made by Parliament and State legislatures. The United Front government will ensure that these laws are implemented in the spirit in which the laws were made. The rights of trade unions will be respected and recognition of trade unions will be required to be done by secret ballot.

Some laws have been made in respect of labour in the unorganised sector. These laws will be strengthened and, where necessary, new laws will be made to protect the interests of such labour particularly in the construction and *beedi* rolling industries.

Infrastructure

Investment in infrastructure has to be stepped up from the present 3.5%–4% of GDP to at least 6% of GDP in the next few years. The economy cannot grow and the needs of the people cannot be met without more capacity in power, oil, telecom, railways, roads and ports. The cumulative requirement of these sectors over the next five years is estimated to be $200 billion (Rs. 7,00,000 crores) at the very minimum. Thus, there is ample room for all modes of investment — public and private, domestic and foreign. The United Front acknowledges that the State and public investment have a leading role to play in the development of infrastructure. The scope, functions and the procedures of the Foreign Investment Promotion Board will be reviewed in order to make it an effective and credible instrument to promote foreign investment in India. Transparent rules and regulations will be drawn up to attract foreign investment and for the award of contracts if any. Every decision on the award of large contracts will be made public together with the process by which the decision was arrived at.

There is a strong link between infrastructure development and financial sector reforms. Infrastructure needs long-term finances. The United Front government will carry out further reforms of the financial sector so that the flow of both domestic and foreign funds to the infrastructure sector is enhanced substantially. There is room for public sector companies and private sector companies to co-exist and compete in the financial sector.

We have gained considerable experience in the working of the banking sector. The said experience will be applied to the restructuring of the insurance industry but at the same time public sector companies like LIC, GIC etc. will be strengthened.

Public Investment

There is a crucial role for public investment particularly in social sectors like education and health. However, organisational and management changes in these sectors are as necessary as increased investment. Besides, there can be no compromise on efficiency and productivity. Public services and utilities must be made to deliver at the lowest cost. Where there is a need for subsidy, the subsidy must be closely targeted to benefit the really needy and the poor.

Fiscal Management

It is recognised world over that fiscal prudence is the key to low inflation, stable price levels and rapid growth. The United Front is committed to bringing the fiscal deficit to below 4% of GDP. The management of the fiscal deficit will, therefore, enjoy the highest priority. The United Front government will continue with tax reforms and take other steps to augment revenues legitimately due to the government and to curb tax evasion. All inessential and unproductive expenditure will be eliminated. Subsidies will be targeted to the really needy and poor. Public borrowing will be severely restricted and, as far as possible, borrowed money will not be used for consumption expenditure. Growth in domestic debt will be slowed down and a portion of the debt will be retired in a phased manner. These principles of fiscal management will, however, not be followed at the cost of development or investment.

Price Stability

The Public Distribution System will be strengthened to meet the twin objectives of price stability and making available essential articles to the poor. Special cards will be given to families below the poverty line and essential articles under the PDS will be sold to them at one-half of the normal issue prices. Access to the PDS will be barred for the affluent sections of the society. While the responsibility of supplying foodgrains and essential articles will remain with the Central and State governments, the management of PDS shops will be entrusted to elected Panchayats and Nagar Palikas.

Foodstocks and foreign exchange reserves will be used imaginatively and purposefully to stabilise prices. Speculators, hoarders and blackmarketeers create havoc with availability and prices of essential articles. Preventive and punitive action will be taken against them. Swift and severe punishment will be meted out to the offenders.

Drinking Water, Primary Healthcare and Housing

Although drinking water, primary healthcare and housing are subjects which fall under the purview of the State governments, the Central needs of every citizen are satisfied. Special plans will be drawn up during the Ninth Plan period to ensure that:

- (i) every habitation has access to potable drinking water;
- (ii) one primary health centre is established for a population of 5,000 people and it is efficiently managed; and
- (iii) the very poor have access to houses built under the public housing programme or to credit that can be utilised to build their own houses so that the goal of providing a shelter to every family is achieved by the year 2005.

Education

Six percent of the nation's GDP will be earmarked for education. This will be achieved by the year 2000. 50% of these funds will be spent on primary education. Substantial funds will be earmarked for imparting technical and vocational skill and training in order to turn out more employable and self-employed youth. The goal of the National Literacy Mission to cover 10 crore adults will be achieved by the target year 1998–1999. The NLM will give special attention to the spread of literacy among women.

The United Front is also committed to making the nation fully literate by the year 2005. A special effort will be made in the States where there is very high incidence of illiteracy and constitute the bulk of educational deprivation. Weaknesses and loopholes in the implementation of the literacy programme will be identified and removed.

The mid-day meal scheme will be implemented in all the States to ensure regular attendance and retention in primary and middle schools. In every initiative that is taken to promote the spread of education, the girl-child will be a special focus of attention.

Science & Technology

Science and Technology are engines of change and growth. A nation can ignore the advances made in science and technology only at its peril. All-out efforts, including the provision of adequate funds, will be made to promote research and development and to strengthen the national and other laboratories. The United Front government will adopt and implement a forward looking policy on science and technology which will help build a modern and self-reliant society on the foundations of a rational outlook, scientific temper, creative work and material progress.

Clean Administration

The United Front is committed to a corruption-free and clean administration. A Bill to set up the Lok Pal will be introduced in the first Budget session of the 11th Lok Sabha. The Bill will cover the office of Prime Minister as well. All Members of Parliament will be required by law to declare their assets annually before the Lok Pal.

The Official Secrets Act will be reviewed and amended keeping in tune with the need for openness and transparency in governance. A Bill on Freedom of Information will be introduced within six months to give the people access to information at all levels.

Discretionary quotas, hitherto enjoyed by Ministers, will be abolished. In areas where it is necessary to make a small number of out-of-turn allotments, such allotments will be made by a Committee and in accordance with published rules and guidelines. All exercise of discretionary powers in this behalf will be made public quarterly through a suitable publication equivalent to the gazette.

A Bill on electoral reforms reflecting the consensus already arrived at will be introduced in the first Budget session of the 11th Lok Sabha.

A Bill on judicial reforms will be introduced within six months in order to expedite trial of cases and to eliminate delays.

In consultation with the Chief Justice of India and the Chief Justices of High Courts steps will be taken to dispose of all pending cases within a period of three years.

The United Front government is committed to fight corruption, particularly corruption in high places, and will take such steps as are necessary and in accordance with the law to restore the confidence and credibility of the offices and institutions of the State.

The people of the country are greatly exercised by the growing emergence of a nexus between politicians, civil servants, businessmen and criminal elements which has been eloquently illustrated by the report of the Vohra Committee. The United Front government will disclose to Parliament the relevant facts and material which formed the basis of the report of the Vohra Committee. It will also set up a statutory authority with adequate powers to go into these facts and circumstances and make suitable recommendations to identify and punish the guilty with a view to eliminate the role of the "parallel government".

Jammu and Kashmir

The State of Jammu and Kashmir and its people are an inalienable part of India. The resolution of the problem of Jammu and Kashmir can only be through consulting the wishes of the people. The elections held recently from 6 Lok Sabha constituencies is a first step in the process of consultation. The United Front is committed to hold elections to the Jammu and Kashmir State Legislative Assembly as soon as possible. Respecting Article 370 of the Constitution as well as the wishes of the people, the problems of Jammu and Kashmir will be resolved through giving the people of that State the maximum degree of autonomy.

Assam and the North-Eastern States

The problem of influx of foreigners into Assam will be resolved on the basis of the Assam Accord to which the Central government is a signatory. The resolution of the issues relating to ULFA and Bodo Security Force also lies only through a political dialogue.

The United Front government will take up special programmes for the economic development of Assam and the North-Eastern region. The recrudescence of insurgency in Manipur, Mizoram and Nagaland is a cause for concern and will be met with a firm resolve to enforce law and order.

Foreign Policy

There is a large measure of consensus on foreign policy which is based on our traditional values and on the experience gained during the freedom struggle and in the post-independence era. Non-alignment is the cornerstone of our foreign policy. The United Front government will closely adhere to the consensus.

Good and friendly relations with neighbouring countries will receive the highest priority. The SAARC forum and SAPTA leading to SAFTA will be the principal instruments through which close and friendly relations will be forged between India and her South Asian neighbours.

China is a neighbour of India. Important steps were taken in recent years towards cordial relations and harmony between India and China. Further steps will be taken in this direction.

The United Front government will work to strengthen the Non-Aligned Movement. It will also actively participate in the deliberations of UNCTAD so that the organisation and the member countries are able to articulate the views of the developing countries.

India has taken many initiatives to become a partner in many multilateral arrangements e.g. the Indian Ocean Rim, APEC and ASEAN. These initiatives will be pursued.

While India has good relations with all countries of the world, it has especially warm relations with the United States and Russia as well as Japan and many countries in Central Asia, South East

Asia, the European Union, the Middle East, Africa and Latin America. These warm relationships will be emphasised while strengthening relations with all countries of the world.

The United Front government will continue the South-South dialogue in order to make South-South cooperation an important plank of multilateral efforts taken by the developing countries.

The United Front government will continue to work for universal nuclear disarmament and will retain the nuclear option till this goal is achieved. It will press India's case for permanent membership of the Security Council.

Economic and commercial relations are now important components of our foreign policy. Foreign economic relations will be based on the principle of mutual cooperation and benefit through bilateral and multilateral arrangements.

International Bodies and Treaty Obligations

India has been an active member of the United Nations since its inception. India is also a founder of many international bodies and organisations. These organisations will play an important role in an increasingly interdependent world. The United Front government will assert India's rights and interests in these organisations. It will also mobilise other developing countries to fight for their rights. In forging international or multilateral agreements, the United Front government will continue to ensure the interests of the country's agriculture, leading sectors of industry and our genetic resources.

Prasar Bharati Act

The Prasar Bharati Act will be reviewed and amended in the light of the recent judgements of the Supreme Court and implemented without further delay.

Environment

The United Front is committed to protecting and preserving the environment and the adoption of green policies in every walk of life. A massive programme for afforestation, wasteland development and revegetation of degraded forests will be launched through Panchayati Raj institutions.

The United Front government's policy on environment will be consistent with the need for rapid and sustainable economic development. Stern measures will be taken against pollution and polluters. The interests of the workers will be safeguarded when it becomes necessary to relocate polluting industrial units. The displacement of communities as a result of developmental activities will be avoided as far as possible and, in any case, rehabilitation of the displaced families will be made an integral component of any developmental plan.

Millions of young men and women are imbued with idealism. The United Front government will harness the energies of the youth. They will be recruited in Development Corps and deployed in a large number of public works like afforestation, repair and restoration of canals, waterways and irrigation systems etc.

Conclusion

India today is in the midst of a major transition in its economic, social and political life. This is a transition period which will be guided by the need to strengthen the principles of democracy, secularism, federalism and social justice. The ethos of our humanist tradition and the aspirations of the Independence struggle inspire the United Front government to carry out the above programme. In the building of this new India of equality, justice and fraternity, we seek the fullest participation of all citizens. The hallmark of the United Front government's approach will be the greater and greater involvement of our people in all its endeavours.

From Visionary Nehru to Gowda

Press Trust of India carried an interesting and quite informative story, giving a short description of each Prime Minister, right from Jawaharlal Nehru to the present Prime Minister, H.D. Deve Gowda. The same is reproduced below. We hope the learned readers will find this piece of information quite interesting and valuable too.

From Visionary Nehru to contractor Gowda, India sees 12 PMs

From the Cambridge-educated, liberal-leaning Nehru to the simple civil-contractor turned politician H.D. Deve Gowda, the country has seen 12 Prime Ministers since Independence.

Shastri, Indira Gandhi, Morarji Desai, Charan Singh Rajiv Gandhi, V.P. Singh, Chandra Shekhar, Narasimha Rao and Vajpayee, the Prime Ministers have come from the North West and South of the country, leaving only the East alone so far.

These men and women of India's destiny ranged from the visionary Nehru to the stern, spartan Desai, from the humble Shastri to the courageous and impatient Indira Gandhi, from rustic Charan Singh to the modern Rajiv Gandhi, from socialist Chandra Shekhar to V.P. Singh, the votary of social justice.

From erudite Narasimha Rao and poetic Vajpayee to the earthy Gowda, the one-time road contractor who has laid a political path all the way from a village in Hassan in Karnataka to the Prime Ministerial office in about four decades of political life.

Nehru: Prime Minister from August 15, 1947 till his death on May 27, 1964, Pandit Nehru had the longest Prime Ministerial innings so far.

A visionary, fired by modern ideas Nehru dreamt of transforming the feudal land into a modern, welfare state and called the nation's nascent industries "the temples of modern India."

In his famous tryst with destiny speech on the midnight of August 14/15, 1947, Nehru gave expression to his dreams thus: "we have to build the noble mansion of a free India where all her children may dwell."

Shastri: Prime Minister between June 1964 and January 1966, Lal Bahadur Shastri left his imprint as a leader with uncompromising honesty and integrity.

He gave the inspiring slogan *Jai kisan, jai jawan* during the 1965 war with Pakistan and displayed his quite courage in those difficult days.

He died in Tashkent during peace talks with Pakistan President Gen. Ayub Khan in January 1966.

Indira Gandhi: Nehru's darling daughter, Indira Gandhi had two spells of office — from January 1966 to March 1977 and from January 1980 till her assassination on October 31, 1984.

Courageous and controversial Indira drew admiration and arraignment in equal measure. She won unadulterated admiration when she led the country to victory in the "Bangladesh war" forced on India by Pakistan in December 1971 but became almost an object of hate for her Emergency rule between June 1975 and March 1977.

She was gunned down by her own Sikh security guards.

Morarji Desai: A stern Gandhian. Desai was perhaps the most harassed Prime Minister by his own men in the Government.

Heading the Janata Party regime comprising men of disparate backgrounds and idealogies, Desai resigned in just over two years in August 1979 the moment he knew he had lost his majority.

Though controversial, Desai's integrity and honesty were never in doubt and was awarded a Bharat Ratna like Nehru, Indira and Rajiv.

Desai followed spartan ways and using natural therapy, enjoyed good health almost in the end and nearly completed 100 years of life.

Charan Singh: A kisan at heart and outlook, the veteran politician from Uttar Pradesh, went down in history with the dubious distinction of being a Prime Minister who never faced Parliament.

He became the Prime Minister after the fall of the Desai Government with promised support from the Congress in August 1979, but resigned within days when the Congress withdrew support suddenly and became the caretaker Prime Minister till the elections at the end of the year. He died in 1987.

Rajiv Gandhi: At 41, Rajiv Gandhi was the youngest Prime Minister and led his party to a big win in 1985. After a euphoric year or two, problems like the Bofors gun deal and the rebellion of his Finance Minister V.P. Singh began plaguing Rajiv.

Not surprisingly he lost the November 1989 poll. He was assassinated in the midst of 1991 elections, without realising his dream of taking the nation to the 21st century.

V.P. Singh: Prime Minister for 11 turbulent months from December 1989 to November 1990, V.P. Singh is best remembered for his controversial decision to accept the recommendations of the mandal commission, which was in limbo since 1978. He resigned in November 1990 when the BJP withdrew support to his minority Government.

Out of Government in the last six years, Mr. Singh still remains an enigma to many.

Chandra Shekhar: Taking over from Mr. Singh, the former "Young Turk" from Balia, was in office for seven months. His Government fell in March after Congress withdrew support to his minority Government.

Narasimha Rao: Heading yet another minority Government, the patient and shrewd Rao gradually transformed it into a majority Government with deft political moves that saw people like Mr. Ajit Singh, the former Janata Dal leader, joining Congress.

Though rocked by scandals and internal dissension, with his bete-noir Arjun Singh, leading the rebel ranks and breaking away. Mr. Rao completed a full term in office.

Vajpayee: Taking over as the 11th Prime Minister on May 16 after 1996 general elections, the liberal and litereatuer, Vajpayee excited the entire nation by deciding to form Government with the support of less than 200 MPs in the 543-member Lok Sabha. He resigned on May 28.

Deve Gowda: The dramatic development pitchforked the 63-year-old Deve Gowda, a hitherto state politician, into the nation's highest executive office as the 12th Prime Minister.

Courtesy: *Pioneer*, 2.6.1996

Books on Deve Gowda

Within a short span of six months since Deve Gowda became the Prime Minister three books have been written on him, which made headlines. The books are:

1 Gowda-Ahmadi, The Midnight Meet? Author: Dr. Janak Raj Jai
2 Deve Gowda King of Corruption
3 From order to Anarchy and politics and Economics of the United front Government Author: Dr. K. Venkatagiri Gowda

All these books have created lot of controversy. A Case has been filed by the son of the Prime Minister against the author in a local court for publishing defamatory material against the Prime Minister.

As regards the second and the third book, the author Dr. Venkatagiri was arrested and later on released on bail. In a press statement the author told the media that he had received threats to his life. The news as appeared in the *Pioneer* dated 7-12-96 is reproduced below.

Gowda-basher arrested, freed

Leading Economist Prof. K. Venkatagiri Gowda has charged Prime Minister H.D. Deve Gowda and his two sons with master-minding his arrest.

Prof. Venkatagiri was arrested on Friday by the Bangalore city police for "publishing defamatory material against the Prime Minister and inciting violence and riots." He was later released on bail by the Jayanagar police.

Prof. Venkatagiri, who is a former MP, said: "The Prime Minister may have instructed his sons to have me arrested."

He said: "They cannot control my thought process or dictate what I should write or should not write. If my writing is defamatory, let them go to the court, I would rather go to the gallows than apologise."

Prof. Venkatagiri, who retired as the head of the economics department of Bangalore University, recently published two books, (1) H.D. Deve Gowda, "The King of Corruption" and (2) From Order to Anarchy, Politics and Economics of the United Front Government". He said he would file a criminal case against the Prime Minister's son H.D. Kumaraswamy, MP, for writing a threatening letter to him. Prof. Venkatagiri said that Mr. Kumaraswamy had recently written a letter to him asking him to make a public apology or face the "consequences within a week". He recalled that exactly one week ago he received a letter purportedly written by Mr. Kumaraswamy.

On why the books did not bear the addresses of the printers, he said that the printer feared trouble and declined to give the address. "After all, I am the publisher and I shall take responsibility for everything I have written," he added.

He said he had already sent letters to the President of India and the Chief Justice of India on the danger to his life being posed by Mr. Kumaraswamy and the Prime Minister's other son and Karnataka housing minister H.D. Revanna. He said he had mentioned in the letter that he would be "glad to die a natural death than an unnatural one."

A Bangalore court has already given interim direction against the re-publication, translation and circulation of the two books.

The Jayanagar police had registered a suo motu case against him under Section 153, 501, and 504 of the Indian Penal Code..

Besides, cases have been registered under the Press and Registration of Books Act.

An Editorial under the title — "Gowda vs. Gowda' as published in *The Times of India* dated 11.12.1996 is as under:

Gowda vs Gowda

The arrest of economist and former MP K. Venkatagiri Gowda, on the orders of a Bangalore court, is a case of excessive enthusiasm to suppress a fundamental right — the freedom of expression. Mr. Gowda's fault was that he had written and published two books which had "derogatory references" to Prime Minister Deve Gowda. The court issued a bailable warrant of arrest against the victim under the Press and Registration Act on the ground that the publication and distribution of the books were likely to incite violence. Not entirely surprisingly, the petitioner was the Prime Minister's son. The books in question which bore the titles — H.D. Deve Gowda-King of Corruption and Unmaking of India; and from Order to Anarchy: Politics and Economics of the united Front Government — are apparently neither great pieces of investigative reporting nor a researcher's delight. In fact, they don't even mention the names of the publisher and the printer. But then, the merit of the work and its authenticity are not the issues here. What is at issue is the knee-jerk, and, indeed, arbitrary reaction to executive criticism, though arguably slanderous in this case. If it was a private case, we would have asked that the target of attack file a defamation or a libel suit. But where the case involves a public authority, a position which necessarily carries with it the risk of public scrutiny and criticism, even recourse to such a step is quite unnecessary.

Certainly, there can be no case for the arrest of an author critical of those in power. Individual criticism of the executive is, after all, the sine qua non of democracy. In this respect, one recalls with admiration the response of Winston Churchill to the onslaughts of Malcolm Muggeridge on the former's strategy and manipulative tactics. Churchill just refused to intervene. Similarly, numerous American presidents have been the butt of jokes of columnists and political analysts, but rarely have the commentators been harassed. Banning of books and arrest of individuals for criticism of the chief executive run against the very grain of democracy. In fact, the right to know, access to greater information and the attainment of more and more freedoms for the individual were the promises of the Common Minimum Programme of the United Front government. The tradition of checks on the arbitrary powers of the executive, too, has formed the very basis of coalition government since 1977. If Prime Minister Gowda is not a 'super Sukh Ram', as the author claims, nor has his family amassed "colossal assets", as the books allege, then he has nothing to fear. The criticism that Mr. Deve Gowda is the "chief minister of India and the Prime Minister of Karnataka" has certainly not been levelled for the first time. If the Prime Minister wants to dispute the charge levelled by this seemingly 'cranky' professor — trained in the London School of Economics and expelled by the BJP —then he should face them by coming out with the truth rather than put his son up to filing a petition.

Another piece under the Caption-Smear Campaign' as published in *Outlook'* dated 18-12-1996 is given below:

Smear Campaign — A book 'exposing' Deve Gowda is banned by the High Court

There was very little in common between a rustic, first-time member of the legislative assembly and a Ph.D. holder in economics from the London School of Economics. But though the economics professor was 10 years older, the two of them were friends since they belonged to the same caste, lived a few blocks away from each other in a middle-class Bangalore residential area, and were both bitten by the ambition bug in equal degree. When the professor retired from his job in university and opted for a political career, the MLA became minister in the state government. The friendship turned sour.

The minister perceived the erudite economist as a threat to his caste vote bank and created hurdles in his path. He was prevented from getting a vice-chancellorship, almost deprived of a state award for meritorious service, and even the specific definition of his caste was distorted, leading to his defeat in a parliamentary election. Or so the economist's supporters claim. The minister's fortunes, meanwhile, took an upswing: he became chief minister and within 18 months of that, Prime Minister.

The economist, cooling his heels after a shattering electoral defeat in his bid for re-election as MP, decided to expose the PM and his alleged misdeeds. The result: a book titled *The King of Corruption and the Unmaking of India*; and a chapter, *H.D. Deve Gowda — A Profile of Corruption, Chicanery, Vindictiveness and Cowardice,* in a second book titled *From Order to Anarchy — Politics and Economics of the United Front Government*. The author; Professor K. Venkatagiri Gowda, 73. The protagonist: H.D. Deve Gowda. But is this fact or fiction? A question that is begging an answer after it triggered a battle of the Gowdas last week even as a Bangalore court virtually banned the two books.

No sooner had the court invited criticism for the "overenthusiastic and strange" ruling, the police swung into action. On December 5, as Janata Dal supporters crowded outside the author's house, the police registered a case under Section 153 and 504 of the Press and Registration Act — on the ground that the publication and distribution of the book was likely to incite violence. Also, the book does not mention the publisher's name (the author himself in this case). The next day, as JD supporters kept up their protests outside, Venkatagiri Gowda was arrested from his Jai Nagar residence, and released in the evening. The battle will now be fought in court, as the PM's sons take up cudgels to protect his reputation.

The drama that promises to pack in lots more action unfolded after excerpts from the two books were published by two leading English dailies and one Kannada daily in Bangalore. The excerpts accused Deve Gowda and his family members of indulging in corruption and nepotism; made fun of the Prime Minister's rusticity and even compared him with politicians caught in the web of scams. The books list some alleged acquisitions of Deve Gowda and his family and even carry pictures of some of them, enough to arouse the ire of the prime minister's sons and some supporters from nearby constituencies.

"Do you expect me to react to that?" an incredulous Deve Gowda asked scribes. His kin thought otherwise. Son H.D. Kumaraswamy, MP. sent a handwritten letter to the retired professor asking him to "prove the charges or tender an apology at a public meeting for making false charges against his father." Thirty-three-year-old H.D. Ramesh, another of Deve Gowda's sons, filed a petition in the second additional city civil court seeking damages and an injunction against the book. And judge A.C. Chandrasekhar issued a temporary injunction restraining the republishing, circulation, distribution, and translation of the two books in the country. This was before the Friday evening swoop.

But Venkatagiri Gowda, a one-term BJP MP who was expelled for "antiparty activities" and returned to the Congress fold, had already ensured that the books reached those it was intended for. Of the 2,000 copies that were printed, over 700 were mailed to all English-speaking MPs, Supreme Court and high court judges, party headquarters and leading newspapers and magazines. So impressed was Deve Gowda's one-time colleague George Fernandes with the book that he flew to Bangalore and ordered 76 copies.

"I am for the politics of integrity and the books are a crusade against corruption. I am willing to produce all evidence if a CBI inquiry is ordered into the allegations," says the outspoken Venkatagiri Gowda who has authored more than a dozen books on economics and counts among his friends former finance minister Manmohan Singh from his days in London.

The Deve Gowda clan is equally belligerent. "How can we defend ourselves from such an attack except by suing the author and seeking a stay on the books?" asks H.D. Ramesh. "We may succeed in fooling people and get away with wrong doings. But we know we'll have to suffer if we sin as we cannot fool the Almighty."

Defamation case filed against author of anti-Gowda books

Hindustan Times, 13.12.96

New Delhi, Dec. 12 The Centre today filed a defamation case in a Delhi court against Dr. K. Venkatagiri Gowda for authoring two books allegedly containing derogatory remarks against Prime Minister H.D. Deve Gowda.

Taking cognizance of the criminal complaint filed by the Centre through special public prosecutor, Mr. K.K. Manan, additional sessions judge, Ms. Indermeet Kaur Kochar, issued summons to Dr. K.V. Gowda and the printers of the two books in Bangalore and listed the case for Dec. 23.

The complaint filed under Sections 500 (defamation), 501 (printing defamatory articles), 34 (common intention) and 120B (Criminal conspiracy) alleged that Dr. K. Venkatagiri Gowda in his two books — 'From Order to Anarchy, Politics and Economics of the United Government' and 'H.D. Deve Gowda (Prime Minister), The King of Corruption and the Unmaking of India' — made allegations for ulterior and mala fide reasons.

Referring to the excerpts of the first book, which says, 'Mr Gowda has been sitting pretty in the South Block on a chair with

13 legs since July 1, 1996, the complaint said that the defamatory statements were in respect of conduct of the Prime Minister in discharge of his duties and functions.

The complaints justified its allegations against the author by referring another paragraph of the book, "It is this helplessness and the resultant loss of authority that has made him deserve the title, 'nincompoop'".

The author cast aspersions on the independence of the three wings of the democracy by intentionally making false allegations against Mr. Deve Gowda.

Quoting from the second book which says "He promises to provide a clean and corruption-free administration knowing fullywell that he was lying to mislead the nation. His administration in Karnataka and Delhi are unclean and corrupt." The complaint alleged that the books contain innumerable imputations calculated to harm the image of the Prime Minister.

The complaint submitted that the accused knew fully well that his act constituted a serious criminal offence and still chose to get the books printed and circulated.

"On the perusal of the averments made in the complaint and the documentary evidence filed along with, that is, the two books, I am satisfied that there is prima facie material to summon the accused persons," the judge said in her order.

The Centre alleged that the books have been printed and published for the sole purpose of circulating the same free of cost among the masses.

It said "the books were circulated among Parliamentarians, officials in the Prime Minister's Office and other persons in authority at New Delhi, and have also been circulated with impunity amongst several other sections of the society in Delhi, where Prime Minister resides and functions, with intention to harm and damage his reputation."

Mr. Manan annexed both the books along with the complaint saying the defamatory statements and imputation made in the books were in such a large measure that the same could not be individualised or itemised in this complaint.

The complaint further said that the relevant and impugned portion/passages for the purpose of prosecution of Dr. K.V. Gowda and others would be proved at the time of recording of evidence.

Defamation Suit against Author of Book on Gowda

Economic Times, 13.12.96

The Centre today filed a defamation case in a Delhi court against Mr. K. Venkatagiri Gowda, a former member of the Lok Sabha, for authoring two books allegedly containing derogatory remarks against prime minister H.D. Deve Gowda.

Additional sessions judge Indermeet Kaur Kochar, who took cognisance of the criminal complaint filed by the Centre, issued summons to Mr. Venkatagiri Gowda and the printers of the two books at Bangalore.

The case will come up for hearing on December 23.

The complaint was filed under Section 500 (defamation), 501 (printing defamatory articles), 34 (common intention) and 120B (criminal conspiracy) of the IPC against the author and M/s Mudrika Printers and M/s Murali Printers.

"On the perusal of the averments made in the complaint and the documentary evidence filed alongwith, that is, the two books, I am satisfied that there is prima facie material to summon the accused persons," the judge said in her order.

The Centre's counsel-pointed out the author in the two books, *'From order to anarchy — politics and economics of United Front government'* and *'H. D. Deve Gowda — the King of corruption and the unmaking of India'*, had alleged certain things which were highly defamatory and derogatory and against Mr. Deve Gowda.

The complaint further said the averments made in these two books denigrated the "esteemed office of the prime minister of India".

The two books were first published on October 2 and October 31, this year.

The Centre alleged the books have been printed and published for the sole purpose of circulating the same free of cost among the masses. It said: "The books were circulated among parliamentarians, officials in the prime minister's office and other persons in authority in New Delhi, and have also been circulated with impunity amongst several other sections of the society in Delhi, where the prime minister resides and functions, with the intention to harm and damage his reputation and defame him in respect of his discharge of public functions."

BJP turns PM's Friend but Only to Corner him

Economic Times, 13.12.96

The Bharatiya Janata Party today turned into a friend of its bete noire, Prime Minister Deve Gowda, but only to embarrass him.

The principal opposition party, which has not spared a single opportunity to target the prime minister today changed track in the Lok Sabha when its member Lalmuni Chaubey took cudgels on behalf of Mr. Deve Gowda over "derogatory" references to the prime minister in a book authored by a former BJP MP, Mr. Venkatagiri Gowda.

Mr. Chaubey, who took up the issue in the Lok Sabha during zero hour, said Mr. Venkatagiri Gowda's book, *H.D. Deve Gowda — the King of corruption and unmaking of India*, was a cause of concern as the writer has labelled the prime minister an undesirable element. "The book has questioned the ethics of legislators. It is a clear case of breach of privilege," he said.

But the Janata Dal members could see through the game of the BJP member, when he freely used the expressions that were used by the author of the book to describe the prime minister.

The JD members, who protested against allowing Mr. Chaubey to raise the issue, said there was a stay on the circulation of the book. "The BJP is indulging in a slanderous campaign against the prime minister," they said.

Speaker P.A Sangma, who intervened, told Mr. Chaubey that his notice was not in order as it was not accompanied by the relevant document.

But Mr. Chaubey was not disappointed with the result of his labour as the speaker said he was free to give a fresh notice along with the document.

For the BJP, it means another day to focus on the personal conduct of the prime minister.

Sangma Refuses Permission to Raise Gowda Book Issue

Indian Express, 13.12.96

Speaker P.A. Sangma rejected permission in the Lok Sabha today to raise the question of a book carrying corruption charges against Prime Minister H.D. Deve Gowda.

During zero hour, the Speaker told Lalmuni Choubey (BJP), who had given the notice, that he rejected the notice as it was not in order.

According to the procedure, the notice should have been accompanied by the relevant document, the Speaker told him, specifying that it was rejected not on merit but on procedural ground.

ENS adds from Bangalore

Meanwhile, Venkatagiri Gowda, a former MP, has asked the State Director General of Police to arrest H.D. Kumaraswamy, MP and son of the Prime Minister.

In a letter to the DGP, copies of which were released to the Press, Venkatagiri said, "I would have been extremely happy if the police had registered a case against Kumaraswamy and others for threatening to take away my life. . . However, it is a pity and a sad day for the people of Karnataka that the police have promptly registered a *suo motu* case against me and have arrested me. . .".

Holding that "many" people were happy that he had "exposed" the Prime Minister, Venkatagiri said that it was only natural that the books — *The King of Corruption* and *The Unmaking of India* — had incited them (Kumaraswamy and others) and no one else.

Venkatagiri said that he had received a letter from Kumaraswamy on December 1 but did not attach importance to it. However, there were anonymous threatening calls which led him to believe that Kumaraswamy's "threat" may be carried out.

PIL Petitions against Deve Gowda

Not only this as many as six writ petitions had been filed in different High Courts of the country challenging the appointment of the Prime Minister Deve Gowda. All the writ petitions have been disposed of in view of the latest Judgment of the Supreme Court in S.P. Anand's Case. One special Leave Petitions — Dr. Janak Raj Jai vs. Shri H.D. Deve Gowda and others had been pending in the Supreme Court, when the petition of S.P. Anand was heard. But the Supreme Court chose not he hear Dr. Jai's petition alongwith S.P. Anand's petition.

After Deve Gowda had met the Chief Justice of India, while the petition against him was pending in the Supreme Court, Dr. Jai wrote a letter to the Chief Justice praying that his Lordships the Chief Justice of India, should not hear tha petition.

Inspite of the said letter, the special Leave Petition was heard on 24.1.1997 by a Bench comprising Chief Justice A.M. Ahmadi, Sujata Manohar and Patnaik. By an order dated 24.1.1997, the Supreme Court dismissed the special Leave Petition.

Walking the Tightrope

Rajat Sharma

A Close friend of H.D. Deve Gowda was telling me the other day, "Whenever I see the Prime Minister, I am reminded of Draupadi. She had five husbands. My friend's plight is worse, because he has to put up with demands of 13 partners". Deve Gowda's well-wisher said that he prefers to call his friend 'Draupada'. the analogy may sound crude, but it is very close to the truth. Deve Gowda is a lonely man at the top, his allies making impossible demands, his partners, who are supposed to provide support, actually twisting his arms. The Prime Minister is literally spending sleepless nights.

Two months after becoming Prime Minister, Deve Gowda had said, "We (the United Front) are going to be a well-knit unit with a common minimum programme. There have been no differences or confrontation. If there are minor problems, we will sort them out." Four months later, he was heard asking his fellow party leaders to ignore the criticism by United Front partners, as they're indulging in criticism to protect their own bases.

The fact is that during the last six months, the United Front steering committee has become a super-cabinet. And many of the coalition party leaders are trying to act as super prime ministers. There are several others who are making demands that seem almost impossible to fulfil. Then, there are cases of personal rivalries among them.

Laloo Prasad Yadav, president of Deve Gowda's own party, isn't happy with the Government. He believes enough is not being done to get him out of the fodder scam trap. Laloo is a friend of the Congress President, Sitaram Kesri. And there is speculation that he may join hands with the Congress, if need be. Kesri, on whose support depends the survival of the Deve Gowda Government, has issued open threats to the Prime Minister.

On the issue of the formation of the government in Uttar Pradesh, Kesri wanted Deve Gowda to persuade Mulayam Singh Yadav to support Mayawati for the Chief Minister's office, knowing fully well that no power on earth can make Mulayam accept Mayawati.

On the contrary, Mulayam had been putting pressure on Deve Gowda to desist from making any overtures to the Bahujan Samaj Party. Mulayam wasn't kindly disposed towards the regular visits of C.M. Ibrahim to the residence of Kanshi Ram. He even conveyed his feeling that in all matters related to Uttar Pradesh, his word alone was to count. The Defence Minister has the complete backing of the two communist parties on this issue.

The communists in any case have taken up the task of being the conscience-keepers of the Deve Gowda government. They sound unhappy about almost everything the United Front government has done. They have distanced themselves from th economic policies of the Government, saying: "The United Front should realise that carrying forward the IMF-World Bank framework of policies will lead to popular discontent, as these policies are against people's interest".

In a virtual chargesheet against Deve Gowda, the Communist parties have accused the Government of acting in a manner that fits more appropriately with the Congress and the BJP agenda. Curiously enough, the Congress continues to attack the PM for departing from the policies of the previous regime. Manmohan Singh, for instance, is not happy with the decisions being taken at North Block.

The list of Deve Gowda's problems with his partners is unending. His Home Minister did not approve of Romesh Bhandari being appointed as the governor of Uttar Pradesh. Nor did Indrajit Gupta approve of the extension given to Home Secretary K. Padmanabiah against his wishes. Jyoti Basu is unhappy that Deve Gowda accepted the demand for a separate

Uttarakhand state. It only helped Subhas Ghising reiterate his demand for a separate Gorkhaland.

The Telugu Desam leader and Andhra Pradesh Chief Minister threw tantrums to secure Central funds for his government. M. Karunanidhi, the Tamil Nadu Chief Minister, of course, did not approve of the Prime Minister's meeting with Jayalalitha. His ally G.K. Moopanar, the leader of the Tamil Manila Congress, is upset that the CBI is scrutinising a case relating to his brother-in-law in connection with the Indian Bank scam.

According to one report, Finance Minister P. Chidambaram has also conveyed his displeasure to Deve Gowda at CBI's action against one of Indian Bank's former officials. And the young CPI(M) leader, Sitaram Yechuri, criticised Deve Gowda for taking his family to Harare and Rome during his official visits. Yechuri even questioned the source of funds spent on their trip.

In the midst of all this, full credit must go to Deve Gowda for being the best tightrope-walker. Supported by his Man Friday, C.M. Ibrahim, Deve Gowda has withstood all pressures and survived. And frankly, in the present circumstances it is all that matters. Deve Gowda has refused to be bullied and bulldozed. He repeats at least once in a day. "I did not come here in search of a job. I will go the day they don't want me to head this government." This posture is indeed Deve Gowda's biggest strength.

Courtesy: *Indian Express,* 8.12.1996

National Politics

India Toady has given an indepth story on the various activities of Shri H.D. Deve Gowda after he had taken over as Prime Minister. We gratefully reproduce below the same for the knowledge of the countrymen who have every right to know the transparent functioning of the Government.

Family Travails (Foreign Grants)

For almost six months after he took office, Deve Gowda stayed put at home. Then, in the last one month, he went abroad along with his family on two official visits. Now, back home, Deve Gowda is having to answer uncomfortable question, such as who paid for the travels of his clan. Says Sitaram Yechury, CPI(M) Politburo member: "We don't know the sources of their (Deve Gowda's relatives) income, or what their level of living or what their earning is."

On his visit to Harare for the G-15 meeting, Deve Gowda was just being a good thatha (grandfather). When his eight grandchildren got after him demanding that they too be part of entourage, he simply could not say no. As Deve Gowda says, "They had seen animals only on TV, I wanted to take them, but since I would not have had the time to look after them, I had to take some adult also." To make the dream come true, Deve Gowda himself admits it cost the family $7,400 (Rs 2.60 lakh).

"Every penny has been paid for. My sons and sons-in-law are earning," insists the prime minister, and he is more than willing to show the bills. If that is indeed so many would like to know where such money is coming from. But the prime minister's aides believe that all the fuss is unwarranted, Former prime ministers and presidents, including V.V. Giri and Shankar Dayal Sharma, have taken their families along on state expense.

An official in the Prime Minister's Office (PMO) claimed that on the last day of the World Food Summit, Deve Gowda wanted to leave Rome at noon even though the departure was slated for evening. He was not interested in sight-seeing. But ended up doing precisely that.

By all accounts, the family had fun. In Rome the Gowdas shared the room at the Le Grand Hotel which the host government had made available to the Indian prime minister and his wife. While Deve Gowda was boasting before fellow delegates that he was the only head of government to have actually tilled the land, his wife Channamma, along with other relatives, hired a coach to visit Florence and Pisa in one day. The next day they flew Alitalia economy class to Venice to enjoy a gondola ride. Among them were Deve Gowda's wife's sister, Saraswatiamma, her daughter and son-in-law, besides one of his sons-in-law and a daughter-in-law.

On their return to Rome, the family sauntered into the duty-free area by mistake, to shop. an SPG officer who warned that domestic passengers were not allowed duty-free shopping was brushed aside by an official from the PMO saying. "After all, it is the prime minister's family." That argument, however, cut noice with the Leonardo Da Vincl airport staff. Shopping apart, the Italian jaunt cost the Gowdas $2,900 (Rs 1.04 lakh).

With two trips in 10 days, costing Rs 3.61 lakh, it is not surprising that questions are being asked by even his coalition partners.

"Nobody Bulldozes Me"

It was A Combative Prime Minister H.D. Deve Gowda that met special Correspondent Javed M. Ansari and Senior Editor Raj Chengappa for an hour-long interview at his residence last week. Excerpts:

Q. You appear to be increasingly hemmed in by some parties in the Steering Committee and unable to take important policy decisions.

A. That is not true, As far as my Government is concerned, the Common Minimum Programme (CMP) is the Bible. All the important decisions that my Government has taken are based on the CMP. So we have done nothing unilaterally. There is no question of anybody bulldozing me on an issue or I, them.

Q. But didn't you put off the hike in petroleum prices under pressure from the Steering Committee?

A. No, no, that's not the way it all happened. We have placed the facts before the leaders and the people and the idea is to make them aware. Let there be a public debate. The issue is how to make up for the Rs 15,000 crore deficit in the oil pool. We have to face these ground realities. But it's also true that most political parties try and resist taking unpopular measures.

Q. Your coalition partners accuse you of taking key decisions on your own without assessing its implications or consulting them?

A. Look, even though the prime minister is guided by the CMP and the advice of the Steering Committee, there are situations in which I, as prime minister, must make certain decisions, I cannot be expected to run to everybody's house to get each decision endorsed. The other day I went to Mewat, seeing the situation there I sanctioned Rs 50 crore. Now if I cannot take decisions on the spot to solve people's problems then I have no business being in the position that I am.

Q. The CPI(M) is unhappy over your unilateral decision to grant statehood to Uttarakhand. Basu says it has opened a Pandora's box.

A. To begin with, it wasn't a unilateral announcement on my part. It was the unanimous decision of the Cabinet. This issue cannot be compared with the Gorkhaland issue. The Uttar Pradesh Assembly has twice passed a unanimous resolution granting statehood. What's the furore all about, I can't understand.

Q. You announced the repeal of the Illegal Migrants Act in Assam and your own coalition partner the AGP has criticised you for it?

A. Even here I did not do anything on my own. During my visit to the North-east, a whole lot of people met me and impressed upon me the need to repeal it. In fact, all the political parties, governmental and non-governmental organisations were in favour of removing the Act, except the Jamaat.

Q. But couldn't you have checked with Chief Minister Prafulla Mahanta before announcing it?

A. Mahanta also had agreed to it and was present at the meeting when I announced it. Now all of a sudden there is criticism. If they have a problem now and if people are not keen on in it, then I won't put it through to Parliament.

Q. Your announcement of a review of the OBC list is another instance where one of your ministers even criticised you in the Cabinet for it.

A. I was totally misquoted. There is nothing new in the announcement. V.P. Singhji had declared years ago that there would be a 10 per cent quota for the economically underprivileged. There is a Supreme Court stipulation that the states as well as the Centre set up a commission headed by a judge to review the castes left out of the list. Kesriji set up a commission whose term expired a couple of months ago. All that I said was we are planning to set up the commission. But unfortunately, the media went to town about it.

Q. You also seem to have failed in Uttar Pradesh to get all the secular forces together. Even Romesh Bhandari has been accused of playing politics at your behest.

A. The whole world knows what the real problem in Uttar Pradesh is. There are certain personal problems between the SP and the BSP which have resulted in the present impasse. Yet, despite all this, the BJP has not been able to form the government. Why blame Bhandari for it. Nobody has to date, a month after the elections, submitted a list of their supporters. In such a situation, inviting the single largest party would lead to horse-trading. And you would have ended up with a JMM-type of situation.

Q. Moving to your own Government's performance, the economy has slowed down considerably.

A. We are struggling to improve the economy. In a situation like this, when the reforms are not getting us the kind of money that we imagined they would, resource mobilisation has been a major problem. The most important thing is to find the money to invest in infrastructure like the power sector. Unless we do that, we will not be able to increase our industrial or agricultural production. We have cleared projects worth Rs 72,000 crore but the investment that we have received so far is only Rs 720 crore.

Q. Why has the response been so poor?

A. There are so many problems. We continue to talk in different voices. Look at China, there is only one voice. It is a Communist country, yet it has attracted investment of about $ 120 billion. But the situation here is that we keep talking endlessly. We have to create a congenial climate for investment. The whole system has to change.

Q. Is the problem because you head a 13-party government and they behave like 13 wives pulling in different directions?

A. I don't think that is the problem. It is the system. When P.V. Narasimha Rao was running the government, it was a one-party affair for five years and Manmohan Singh was the finance minister. How much of investment did they get in? What was the result? It's true that at a critical time they were able to find out a temporary solution. But if you look at the broader picture, where was the investment? Raising a loan is not a solution or great economics. Because of the borrowings from the IMF and the World Bank at that juncture, we have had to repay a heavy amount this year. So let's not blame it on the 13-party factor. The problem is deeper.

Q. But a part of the problem does come from your own coalition partners speaking in discordant voices.

A. Every political party has some areas of differences. This was true of the Congress and is even true of the states in which the BJP and JD is in power. Whether it's within my alliance or outside, if by criticising me it helps them with their party cadres and workers, I'm not worried about it.

Q. The Congress, especially its president Sitaram Kesri, has been increasingly critical of your Government. Is it because you have failed to strike the kind of rapport you had with Rao?

A. The relationship with the Congress is not based on my individual equation with leaders. It is a political relationship. The CWC decided to support me to ensure that a secular government was installed at the Centre. That situation continues even today. I have no problems with anybody.

Q. Do you feel the unity moves of the Congress will ultimately destabilise your Government.

A. People are free to join the Congress if it helps strengthen it. Scindia came and told me he is joining. I said go ahead and help the Congress. So did N.D. Tiwariji. As regards how long the Government will last. I am not worried. The day I took oath, I made it clear that it mattered little how long I stayed in government, whether it was five years. What is important is whether I deliver the goods or not.

Q. CPI(M) leader Sitaram Yechury has openly criticised you for taking your family to Harare and home and questioned the source of the funds.

A. I wish he had asked me rather than rushed to the press. Every penny has been paid for by my family members. Each one of my children and my sons-in-law are earning members. Money was withdrawn from their accounts; the dollars were purchased in Bangalore. We have receipts to show everything. When every penny was paid for, what is wrong if I took my grandchildren to see some wildlife?

Q. The question is, was it proper?

A. Propriety and morals are not guided by others but by one's own conscience. The media also cooks up stories of my meeting the chief justice at midnight and my dozing off.

Q. So what time did you meet him?

A. I have no reason to meet him with my face covered at midnight. I met him for dinner at 8 p.m. It was a routine affair to discuss administrative matters. Why does there have to be an ulterior motive to it?

Q. And what's the truth about dozing off at public functions?

A. If I rest my head on my hands, that's not dozing off. Nobody talks of the 18 to 19 hours I put in my job.

Public Interest Litigation

The fundamental rights guaranteed to the people of India under the Constitution of India will be meaningless if they are not interpreted and implemented liberally by the Courts of our Country. The courts are in fact the custodian of the constitution and they have to protect the poorest and the richest alike. The task is himalyan and needs tremendous courage, dedication, wisdom, integrity, patriotism, and strong will to impart Justice to all those who are frightened, frustrated or a group of people suffering injury, poverty or ignorance. The robed men, i.e., the 'Bar' and the 'Bench' owe an onerous duty towards these have-nots and have to create a Third World Jurisprudence for the said Third World Life.

In Justice Krishna Iyer's words: "social justice can never be transformed into a living principle under condition of penury, disability and primiture privations unless social activitists, vigilant expert bodies and crusaders for common causes bring up injustices for Judicial redressal. Public Interest Litigation where the particular party, who moves the 'Court' suffers no personal injury but agitates a grievance common to the Community, is a necessary forensic archery in the procedural armoury." Justice Iyer further observed:

> "If the weak and the meek are to share the resources of our nation, rule of law, in its dynamic, distributive, democratic militancy must occupy the Commanding heights of the Justice system, and become an activist instrument in the hands of the social, economic and political proletariat in its struggle against the three dimensional proprietariate to establish a better human order and juster legal culture."

Therefore, the judicial branch, with innovative genius and imaginative commitment to the founding creed of our democratic, socialist Republic, must interpret, apply and enforce the law in such leaps that the court becomes the sanctuary of hope for the broad spectrum of the handicapped and the victimised. The value revolution emmisioned by the constitution is within our grasp if the three instrumentalities keep their promise. Otherwise the Constitution is the opium of the people, the law a lollipop, and the court a dope.

Locus Standi

Many a time, question of locus standi arose as to who has the entitlement to file a public interest litigation. And this vital question of locus standi has since been answered by the apex court in so many judgments. Locus Standi, therefore, in the jurisdiction of public interest litigation, enforceable under Art. 32, receives the broadest commutation, since the judicial process must embrace victims from various sections of society, and the adversary system needs renovation to suit the genus of poverty jurisprudence.

In Bandhua Mukti Morcha case, justice P.N. Bhagwati observed:

> "Public interest litigation is not in the nature of adversary litigation, but it is a challenge and an opportunity to the Government and its officers to make basic human rights meaningful to the deprived and vulnerable section of the community, and to assure them social and economic justice which is the signature tune of our constitution, the government and its officers must welcome public interest litigation, because it would provide them an occasion to examine whether the poor and down-trodden are getting their social and economic entitlements or whether they are continuing to remain victims of deception and exploitation at the hands of strong and powerful section of the community . . . ."

Suo moto Intervention by Judges

In many cases, the judges Suo moto have taken note of the aggrieved parties and granted the appropriate relief. For instance a Judge of the Gujarat High Court, after having read a letter to the Editor by a widow monitoring her plight because of non-payment of provident fund etc. on husband's death, ordered a show cause notice to be issued without any formalities to Regional Provident Fund Commissioner.

Recently justice Usha Mehra, of Delhi High Court Suo moto issued a show cause notice to the Civic authorities on Dengu deaths in the capital. The notice was issued only on the information she gathered through media reports.

Human Right Activists/Organisations

The Public Interest Litigation is gaining ground day by day. It has come to stay in our country for all times to come. A large number of human right activists including some public spirited organisations have voluntarily come forward to plead for the common causes involving the rights of the weak, meek, hapless and downtrodden. And happily almost all the High Courts including the Supreme Court are favourably inclined to hear such petitions, of course, if filed bonafide and purposefully.

The number of human right activists as also public spirited organisations are increasing manyfold, and those who selflessly spend time, money and energy towards this onerous cause deserve every appreciation. We are happy to learn that T.N. Seshan, who has recently retired as the Chief Election Commissioner of India has shown his inclination to join Anna Hazare in his crusade against corruption.

It is difficult to mention the names of all the human right activists who have dedicated their life for the causes of the have-nots; but to mention a few they are, H.D. Shourie, Kapila Hingorani, Sheela Barse, M.C. Mehta, Vineet Narayan, Rajinder Puri, Indira Jai Singh, Rajinder Sachhar, Shanti Bhushan, Har Dev Singh, V.M. Tarkunde, Swami Agniwesh, O.P. Saxena, S.P. Anand, Pt. Parmanand Katara, A.C. Pradhan and Dr. B.L. Wadhera. To name few organisations these are Common Cause, Bandhua Mukti Morcha, PUCL, PUDR, Hindustani Andolan, Family Conciliation Service Centre and many others.

With the flood of PIL petitions, filed by the great sons of the soil, and the positive approach by the courts, to go to the depth of the mater, the corrupt politicians and bureaucrats at high places stand exposed. The UnitedFront Govrnment is seriously planning to bring suitable amendments in the Prevention of Corruption Act. This is most unfortunate that the powerful corrupt politicians are bent upon changing the basic feature of the Constitution simply to get immunity from the corrupt practices committed by them.

Prime Minister on P.I.L.

It is a matter of great regret, and shame that in his recent utterances, the Prime Minister, H.D. Deve Gowda has criticised the Public Interest Litigation in so many words. Not only this, he went to the extent of calling PIL as a menace, a private interest litigation and a publicity interest litigation. If all that has appeared in media is correct and are the utterances of the Prime Minister, it goes to establish that he has scant regard for the Judiciary. Almost all the sections of the society have depricated the criticism of the Prime Minister and have also condemned the proposal of an amendment in the Prevention of Corruption Act.

Rajinder Puri, a noted Journalist and human right activist has written an open letter to the President; Justice Rajinder Sachhar has written an indepth article condemning the proposed amendment in the Prevention of Corruption Act.

An, open letter by Rajinder Puri to the President of India, and letter to Editor by Aman Lekhi (a budding Advocate) are reproduced below. These are sufficient to show the mind of the people at large against the proposed misadventures of the Gowda government that wishes to disfigure the Constitution by bringing amendment in the Prevention of Corruption Act.

Letter to The Editor

Malice gives sinister motive to the most virtuous of actions — the Prime Minister, Mr H.D. Deve Gowda's sweeping criticism of public interest litigations (PIL) is a case in point.

Criticism, however, comes easier than craftsmanship and it is craftsmanship which the public interest litigation involves. Departing from the individualistic Anglo-Indian mould, with the intention of making access to justice broad-based and people-oriented, the PIL liberalises the concept of locus standi to permit public-minded citizens or organisations with serious concern for conservation of public resources and direction and correction of public power, promote justice in all its facets. Within the parameters of liberalised standing itself are limitations upon its invocation and pro-bono-publico claims alone are entertained. In entertaining PIL, the courts are not exercising extra-constitutional jurisdiction as the litigation is rooted in Article 14, which provides protection against arbitrariness in State action, Article 21, which guarantees a dignified and meaningful life, and Directive Principles of State Policy, recognised as fundamental in governance of the country. And the lowering of standing requirements is not a development peculiar to India alone but can be seen even in the United States and England. Would it not be anomalous to insist, when protected species are shot, that complaints from wardens alone will be received when the wardens themselves may be conspiring with the poachers? What then is the absurdity in entertaining petitions from private individuals against corruption in the Government when those in the Government conspire to keep the same under wraps? Is the Prime Minister apprehensive of courts policing the corridors of power wanting instead to be left free to violate the law? Prejudices of ignorance are more easily removed than prejudices of interest; the first are blindly adopted, the second wilfully preferred. Mr Deve Gowda's distorted description of Public Interest Litigation, it appears, falls in the second category.

Courtesy: *The Pioneer*

Justice Kuldeep Singh on PIL

In a recent discussion on the role of subordinate judiciary, organised by Capital Foundation Society. Justice Kuldip Singh said, "It is absolutely necessary that all the three tiers of the Judiciary are permitted to function independently and the day today interference in the matter of lower courts is uncalled for."

Referring to the current spate of Public Interest Litigation (PIL) Justice Kuldip Singh said the practice would continue to be in vogue till the illiterate and the poor people were not in a position to seek justice for themselves. The views on PIL expressed by Justice Kuldip Singh have been published in almost all the national newspapers of 24.12.1996.

Therefore, those who criticise the Public Interest Litigation are not the friends of the illiterate, poor, hapless and the downtrodden people of our Country.

Note: To know more about Public Interest Litigation please go through the chapter on PIL in a book written by the same author *Compensation under the Motor Vehicles Act. A Critique,* Regency Publications, New Delhi.

Untold Story

The mystry behind the appointment of H.D. Deve Gowda, as the 12th Prime Minister of world's largest democracy has been unfolded in the book: *Jyoti Basu — The authorised biography by Prof. Surabhi Banerjee.*

As revealed in the book even P.V. Narasimha Rao wanted to form the Government at the Centre. The race to form the Government began on 9th May, but for a while it seemed that no party would be able to sink its differences for long enough to achieve a precarious majority... The Third Front hoped that a group of Congressmen might decide to leave the Congress and join a non-Narasimha Rao non-BJP Government. PV Narasimha Rao was trying to garner support so that his depleted congress could stake its claim. The left parties bickered and dithered among themselves, and smaller parties like the Tamil Manila Congress and the Asom Gana Parishad were prepared to be wooed without committing themselves to anyone.

Hectic activities had been going on in the capital, right from 9th May, 1996 to 14th May, 1996, when the President was left with no other option than to invite Atal Behari Vajpayee to form the Government. From the United Front, the names in currency were V.P. Singh, Ram Krishna Hegde, Laloo Prasad Yadav and Jyoti Basu. There were some reservations on the name of V.P. Singh, as Mulayam Singh opposed his name, but there was unanimity on the name of Jyoti Basu. None of the constituents had any objection to this name.

The overall impression created among the people was that Jyoti Basu himself declined the offer was absolutely far from reality. There is no doubt that he was hesitant initially, but looking to the interest of the nation as also his party, he was very much inclined to take this responsibility of heading the Government at the Centre. But his own partymen ditched him, may be out of jealousy or personal rivalries. The CPI(M) thus missed the golden opportunity to rule at the Centre. Basu calls it a historical blunder which his party committed simply to see that Jyoti Basu is not able to adorn the office of Prime Minister. It is unfortunate that personal jealousies, by the so called disciplined party came in the way rather than the national interest. Out of disgust and frustration, it looks that Jyoti Basu suggested the name of Shri H.D. Deve Gowda in his place, which was readily agreed to. The country's fate was, therefore, decided by a person, who himself could not get his name cleared from his own party.

Here is an authorised story of the whole drama that was played to crown the farmer cum contractor cum politician — Shri H.D. Deve Gowda, as the 12th Prime Minister of this great country. In this process, therefore ten million people of this great democratic republic had simply been the silent spectators.

As the days passed, and, the dead-line approached for the new Government to be sworn in, the politicking increased. Both Basu and V.P. Singh would not say yes and the impasse continued. While Basu was still in Calcutta and preparing to leave for Delhi he received a call from Shri V.P. Singh, who told him that the Janata Dal and all others unanimously wanted him as their leader and Prime Minister.

> "It was nice to hear such tidings" says Basu, after a brief pause. But could not commit anything at the moment."

After he reached Delhi, there was spate of calls, which did not cease until well after midnight. Basu spent a restless night. He felt thoroughly tired and restless. He had a clear vision of the unstable future of the Third Front, but at the same time he realized the necessity of holding the BJP at bay. While giving his consent he is on record to say: "Yes, it is for the credibility of the Third Front," he said at the time, "I am ready to offer myself as the consensus candidate, if there is no other alternative, even though my health is not good. However the decision lies with the Central Committee." The politbureau met the next morning and decided not to be a part of the Government. Seeing the mood of the politbureau, Basu got very much disappointed. He then suggested that the matter may be placed before the Central Committee

Basu did not betray his inner turmoil and proposed that as politbureau was undecided, the issue be placed before the Central Committee. The proposals framed for the Central Committee, which was scheduled to meet on 13th May, were whether there should be a non-congress Government at the Centre supported by the Congress from outside (but only unconditionally) and whether the CPI(M) was going to participate in Government. "I waited for the stand of the Central Committee though I could feel their pulse after the politbureau meeting. I rang Mulayam to say that they must look for a new leader. I cannot deny that I felt that we were making a mistake in the new situation."

The Central Committee met on the morning of 13th May. Basu presided over the meeting. Harkishan Singh Surjeet presented a note on the decision in the politbureau and the majority and minority views. The issue sparked off a heated debate which went on for several hours — but the majority was not to join the United Front Government. Basu displayed a calm exterior during the meeting, but a fierce storm was brewing within. In the words of Jyoti Basu — At one point, I thought that we have been patient enough, enough is enough, and it is time to put the issue to the vote — rare occurrence in the history of Central Committee."

The majority voted against joining the Government. Thirty-five votes were cast by the majority against twenty for the minority view while four remained undecided.

Meanwhile, as the Central Committee deliberated the main partners in the Central Committee of the CPI(M) at about 4'O Clock in the evening, most of the leaders criticised the decision. Basu and Surjeet reached Bihar Bhavan at about seven-thirty, with a copy of the decision of the Central Committee. The meeting room was brimming with important political leaders among them Indrajit Gupta, Mulayam Singh Yadav, Laloo Prasad Yadav, I.K. Gujral, Surendra Mohan , Ram Vilas Paswan, and Wasim Ahmad. The decision of the Central Committee of the CPI(M) came to the front as a bolt from the blue. Crisis loomed large. If they could not choose their leader the BJP was going to form the Government. The leaders requested the CPI(M) to reconsider its decision in view of the threat of communalist forces hijacking the Government. Surjeet promised to ask the Central Committee to review its decision. The members of the

Central Committee were immediately informed about the Special Session next morning to review their earlier decision in the light of the appeal by the United Front Leaders . . . The Special Meeting on 14th May stuck to its earlier stand. Discussions ensued until Basu called for votes, but the majority still opposed the proposal to join the Government and make Basu the Prime Minister. Later Basu met with leaders of the United Front and alternative names for the Prime Ministership were discussed. In the absence of Basu and V.P. Singh as candidates, G.K. Moopanar of Tamil Manila Congress and H.D. Deve Gowda were mooted as alternatives. Basu proposed Deve Gowda for the Prime Ministership and this was accepted.

Jyoti Basu, of course, was very unhappy and a sad person as his party did not take a proper decision and asked him not to head the Government.

> "Apparantly it was the lack of porper political understanding, I would say, which stood in their way of reacting positively to the situation," Basu replied. "It was a historical blunder."

Surabhi Banerjee in her book writes that:

> The General feeling following the Central Committee's decision was that it was the age-old internal divisions within the party, and not the natural interest that decided the issue. Many of the Central Committee members had come to the meeting determined not to let Basu become Prime Minister because of personal rivalry and ideological differences. It was with this background that Deve Gowda's name was floated for the Prime Ministership. Since P.V. Narasimha Rao the then Congress President did not send the letter of support in time, the President was forced to invite Atal Behari Vajpayee to form the Government. But since Vaypayee could not prove his majority on the floor of the house, the BJP Government had to be dissolved within 13 days of its installation. And ultimately Deve Gowda adorned the crown of Prime Ministership.

Downgrading the Judiciary

During the six months' misrule of Deve Gowda Government, the institution of Judiciary has been the first casualty. The question arises as to who is to blame people, the judges, the petitions or the bureaucrats? Before we find the answer to this very vital question let us not forget that if the judicial institution is allowed to fail, believe it or not all the other institutions will have no meaning at all. There will be left nothing but chaos, confusion, violence and lawlessness all around and the very existence of this great country will be in great danger.

Political interference with the impartial and independent functioning of judicial institutions e.g. the Supreme Court, High Courts and the subordinate courts must, therefore, be opposed tooth and nail by those who love their country and have any respect for the forefathers of the nation, who brought freedom after laying down their lives fighting the foreign rulers.

On independence of judiciary, let us see what John Rudlege Jr. spoke on the floor of the House of Representatives in 1802:

> "The Government may be administered with indiscretion and violence, offices may be bestowed exclusively upon those who have no other merit than that of carrying votes at the elections, the commerce of our country may be depressed by non-sensical theories and public character may suffer from bad intentions, but so long as we have independent judiciary, the great interest of the people will be safe."

In order to maintain the dignity and independence of the Judicial institution, the Judges also owe an onerous duty to maintain its respectability and impartiality.

The 14th Report of the Law Commission of India, the best ever written by M.C. Setalvad quoted approvingly Winston

Churchil's favourite remarks on the judiciary in the House of Commons of March 23, 1954.

> "A form of life and conduct far more severe and restricted than that of ordinary people is required from judges and though unwritten, has been most strictly observed. They are at once privileged and restricted. They have to present a continuous aspect of dignity and conduct."

The report also contains admonition to Judges in the same vain.

'Midnight Meet': The Much talked about Gowda Ahmadi. The Midnight Meet? brought embarrassment for the institutions—Judiciary as well as the Executive.

Commenting on the most controversial meeting between the Prime Minister and the Chief Justice of India, Mr. A.G. Noorani said:

> "For all one's respect for justice A.M. Ahmadi and his high office, one cannot help saying that he could well have spared himself the embarassment by not meeting the P.M. in the circumstances in which he did, in the first instance, The Judge knows the tradition and conventions of which Deve Gowda is blissfully unaware."

Quoting a distinguished jurist, J. Jafee, Mr. Noorani said:

> "There is real danger of the diminution of public confidence in the courts if it is believed that the judges are in secret communication with the other branch of the Government."

In one of the caveats written by C.R. Irani, Chief Editor, The *Statesman*, had categorically asked the Prime Minister to explain the purpose of his visit to the Chief Justice at a late hour and deny that he had or retains any thought of superseding Mr. Justice Verma either via persuading Chief Justice Ahmadi to take up the National Human Rights Commission or in any other manner.

One of the English Journals observed that by meeting the Chief Justice of India under such circumstances the Prime Minister has downgraded the judiciary. It further observed "The wily politician form Karnataka was never known for politically correct behaviour or adherance to legal proprieties. As Karnataka

Chief Minister he had the audacity to call on the Chief Justice of the High Court in a vain bid to bail out a favourite official who was hauled up for contempt of the Court. He had no qualms of conscience in making use of Reliance aircraft in the Company of liquor baron, Vijay Mallya, when he was the Prime Minister designate to the largest democracy in the world."

> "And now Deve Gowda called on the Chief Justice after the Delhi High Court rejected the Police Commissioners' application for change of venue of P.V. Narasimha Rao's appearance in the Court in Lakhubhai cheating case as a co-accused."

The committee of Judicial accountability comprising legal lumanaries like Shanti Bhushan, Ram Jethamalani, V.M. Tarkunde, D.S. Tewetia, R.B. Mehrotra, Har Dev Singh, Indira Jai Singh and Prashant Bhushan had in a statement described these developments as unfortunate and observed that these had adversely affected the credibility of the Supreme Court and rudely shaken the people's faith in it.

Preface: *Gowda-Ahmadi: the Midnight Meet?*

Here are some exciting revelations by a recently retired, 'Green Judge' of the Supreme Court:

> "The system of judicial appointments should be more transparent, says the former Judge, who wants a national debate on the issue. He points out that Chief Justice controls the High Courts and lower courts by virtue of his power to appoint and transfer Judges. The exercise of his power must be transparent."
>
> Justice Singh feels that his most important jurisprudential contribution was in giving teeth to public interest litigation (PIL). Not content with passing orders, he insisted on monitoring their implementation and put the executive in the dock if it did not comply. "That is judicial activism he says."

Strong on Judicial accountability, he feels justices (and their families) should declare their assets at the time of taking oath and every year thereafter. Chief Justice-designate J.S. Verma, had drafted rules of conduct but Ahmadi was reportedly not enthusiastic. Justice Singh further says, "I am sure Verma will take it up."

On judicial activism the Judge said, "The Parliament is supreme. If they make a law, the judiciary has to accept it but if the law is unconstitutional the Supreme Court will strike it down. The power of judicial review cannot be taken away from the court."

Mr. Singh, disapproves the lower courts tendency to make 'extra judicial comments' about the politicians. At the same time, he says, "they should not get special treatment."

Change of Venue for Narasimha Rao

Justice Kuldip Singh has not taken kindly the Supreme Court decision giving different treatment to P.V. Narasimha Rao by changing the venue of trial at Vigyan Bhavan.

"Setting up a Special Court for former Prime Minister, P.V. Narasimha Rao, was flawed. I would never have passed such an order. You cannot treat different people differently."

(Outlook, January 22, 1997)

Proposed Bill to Curb PIL

Contempt of Court?

The last, but not the least, the Government headed by Deve Gowda, is ready to introduce a Bill in the Parliament, to put stringent restraints on the filing of the Public Interest Litigation. The language used in the draft note sent to the Cabinet, visibly amounts to contempt of court.

Deve Gowda Government is running at the mercy of the Congress, as also the compulsive support of other constituents. He is therefore prisoner of all the constituents and the Congress. To give every facility and protection to all their misdeeds he was prepared to accept an open confrontation with the judiciary even at the cost of committing contempt of Court. He himself has been involved in a number of cases. As many as half a dozen petitions had been filed challenging his appointment as Prime Minster. He was not a member of either House at the time of taking oath as Prime Minster, and had not resigned even from the seat of MLA at that point of time. Maximum number of scams have been exposed in which most of the involved persons belonged to congress. And the Congress (Chief Supporter) is his *maii baap* and *ann daata* (bread and butter giver). So how can Deve Gowda like the judiciary to try them and give any punishment. Every day, the Congress Party comes out with a threat of withdrawing the support. The poor Deve Gowda has to sit knee down before their *aaka* (Master) and accede to their demands — proper or improper, legal or illegal, and moral or immoral.

Proposed draft Bill to Check PIL

The PIL (Public Interest Litigation) and the Judicial activism by the courts, have exposed the real face of the so-called leaders of the country. In order to curb the filing of the petitions containing matters of great public importance by the public spirited persons and the NGOs, the Deve Gowda Government has now come out with a proposed draft bill by which they are intending to completely close the doors of Public Interest Litigation.

Here are some excerpts from *Indian Express* dated 14th February, 1997.

"In a move fraught with far reaching consequences the Deve Gowda Government is considering measure to rein in the judiciary by bringing in a Public Interest Litigation Bill, 1997 in the coming session of Praliament.

A draft of the proposed Bill currently pending before the Cabinet for approval, suggests a mandatory interest free deposit of Rs. 1 Lakh for every Public Interest Litigation in the Supreme Court, and Rs. 50,000 in the High Court. The deposit shall be refunded at the discretion of the court, if the petitioner wins the case.

Among other proposals are the definition of a bonafide public interest litigation, as a person who has some direct personal interest in the litigation, except when it is for the enforcement of the rights of a poor person. The draft defines a poor person as one whose annual income does not exceed Rs. 6,000.

The note to the cabinet states. "The judiciary has digressed from its traditional duties and functions as an interpreter of the Constitution and the laws, and has entered into a field into which it has no competence or safe standards for judicial action."

"Barriers of self restraint and detatchment are becoming thin day by day." The note states, adding that the judiciary "has failed to recognise that it cannot be a substitute for the failure or the irresponsibility of other branches of the Government and start delivering increasingly legislative or administrative judgement."

Simply to hide their own sins, a conspiracy is being hatched to over awe the judiciary, under the garb of bringing a Bill to curb PIL and the frivilous petitions. Our courts are quite competent to decide as to which petition is a frivilous one and should not be entertained. There is thus no need of bringing such a useless Bill.

The people should gird up their loins to oppose this proposed Bill tooth and nail to save democracy and the judicial institution.

O Countrymen
Freedom of the nation is in great peril
Let us save it with all our might.

Prime Minister with no Mandate

Prime Minister, Shri H.D. Deve Gowda, even after seven months or so after his appointment as Prime Minister has not been able to get a mandate from one Parliamentary Constitutency. Still he claims to be ruling the hearts of 100 crores people of the country. He is popularly called Chief Minister of India and Prime Minister of Karnataka.

The name of H.D. Deve Gowda was not sponsored by his own party — Janta Dal — which itself was a truncated group of M.P.s of divided interests. The topmost names in currency in the Janata Dal, were Raja Vishwa Nath Pratap Singh, Ram Krishna Hegde and Laloo Prasad Yadav. When these names were considered or sponsored for the office of the Prime Minister, the name of Deve Gowda was not even in a liquid form. It was the CPI(M) which gave birth to this name, and that too for their own axe to grind. No one had the slightest interest for the country in the topmost storey of their mind.

The topmost leaders of Janata Dal including Shri V.P. Singh, wanted Jyoti Basu to adorn the office of the Prime Minister. Their main aim was that under no circumstances BJP should be able to form the Government at the Centre. And, the CPI(M) wanted that neither the Congress nor the BJP should form the Government. Still they agreed to this extent that they could tolerate the Congress support from outside. The Congress shamelessly gave their consent to this humiliated arrangement. Arithmetically, CPI(M) considered Congress a sworn enemy inside the Government, but an ally outside the Government with the condition that they would abide by conditions laid down in the Common Minimum Programme.

After having agreed on these terms and conditions the name of Jyoti Basu was sponsored probably by Shri V.P. Singh. And after the meeting of the Central Committee at New Delhi, Jyoti Basu declined the offer. And it was Jyoti Basu, who gave birth to the name of Deve Gowda, which was ultimately accepted by all the constituents of the United Front, including of course the Congress, who were just tail enders and silent spectators with no conscience whatsoever. So the fate of the people, as to who should govern them was decided by a coterie of truncated group of leaders, who were not even the elected representatives. What a shame! There is nothing personal against the gentleman, but since it concerns the welfare of the country to which I belong, it has to be everybody's concern that a person who leads the country, must be the elected representative of the people, and should have the unconditional support and confidence of the majority of the Lower House. That is what is the letter and spirit of the Constitution. H.M. Seerval an outstanding Constitutional expert depricated the appointment of Charan Singh as Prime Minister in his book 'Constitutional Law of India Vol. II (Epilogue)' which was made by the then President under similar circumstances.

In this case, the name of Deve Gowda was suggested by Jyoti Basu, (whose party has never gone beyond 2 to 3 states in the country), and was cleared secretly by some likeminded Members of the Janata Dal. Ram Krishna Hedge, who was one of the topmost earlier names for this office and was a very senior leader was not even informed of this most crucial meeting where his name was approved for Prime Ministership. Not only this, when he made certain critical remarks on the behaviour and the functioning of the party leaders, he earned expulsion from his own one time disciple Deve Gowda. Another prominent elected member of Parliament from Janata Dal, Mrs. Maneka Gandhi was also sacked for her calling a spade a spade, criticising the formation of the cabinet by Deve Gowda.

The President of India, Dr. Shankar Dayal Sharma, was very much in the know of all these developments. He had also the knowledge of the working of the earlier Governments headed by persons belonging to a minority party. The President was also aware that these 13 parties which had joined together could not give a clean and stable Government, but had joined hands to keep at bay the BJP, and the communists wanted to oust Congress in the same scale. On the curcial day, the President was informed that they would produce the letter of support from the Congress President P.V. Narasimha Rao, by 1.30 P.M. and the President agreed to their demand. Rashtrapati Bhawan had been virtually surrounded by the journalists, photographers, and the Electronic Media. Upto 3.55 P.M. the letter of support from Shri P.V. Narasimha Rao did not reach.

President Invites BJP

The President was thus left with no other choice than to invite the BJP, the largest single party. Therefore Atal Behari Vajpayee was installed as the Prime Minister with a direction to prove his majority on the floor of the House. The letter of support from Congress reached very late and the President could nto wait for the letter indefinitely.

The Janata Dal leaders became very furious and misbehaved with the President when he had invited Atal Behari Vajpayee to form the Government. The President kept cool and did not react. When Atal Behari Vajpayee could not prove his majority on the house, he straight away went to Rashtrapati Bhawan and gracefully handed over the resignation of his Government. Inspite of the bad blood created by the Janta Dal and the United Front, by accusing him earlier, the President invited Shri H.D. Deve Gowda to form the Government and asked him to prove the majority on the floor of the House.

Taking into consideration all the events that have been narrated can we say that there existed subjective satisfaction of the President to invite Deve Gowda to form the Government?

Legally we may not be able to successfully challenge the subjective satisfaction of the President of India, but we have every right to express our feelings publicly that if the President had kept in view the fate of earlier Governments of Ch. Charan Singh and Chandra Shekhar, the country would have been saved from such a precarious situation. I have highlighted all the situations in my earlier work "Commissions and Omissions by Indian Prime Ministers"

Here are some excerpts from the said book as mentioned in a review published in Alive — (formerly known as Caravan) August, 1996.

"After Morarji's resignaion, President Sanjeeva Reddy invited Y.B. Chavan to try and form a Government. But Chavan failed to explore the offer and wrote to Charan Singh that 'The Congress Party in Parliament whose strength in Lok Sabha is 75, will support you in your endeavour to form a Government.

Both Morarji and Charan Singh staked their claims to form a Government and both worked very hard to procure outside support.

Morarji's list Contained Bogus names

Morarji wanted one more day to show his strength of Members of Parliament but the President declined as he felt that it was not proper to give more time to Morarji than to Charan Singh. After a careful scrutiny and examination, the President came to the conclusion that Charan Singh had the support of the majority of M.P.s.

It was later found that some bogus names were included in the list submitted by Morarji's side. This allegedly embarrassed Morarji to such an extent that he resigned from the leadership of Janata Parliamentary Party.

On the 28th July, 1979, Charan Singh was sworn in as Prime Minister alongwith Y.B. Chavan as Deputy Prime Minister with the support of Indira Gandhi (who was his sworn enemy). Charan Singh was visibly happy and announced before the television cameras "My life's ambition has been fulfilled."

By this Charan Singh allowed himself to be trapped well and proper in the net that Indira Gandhi had laid for him. According to Madhu Limaye, the President confided that when the first crisis broke in the month of July 1979, at her very first meeting with him, Indira Gandhi made it clear that what she was aiming at was a mid-term poll. Her support to Charan Singh was a stop-gap arrangement.

Chandra Shekhar telephoned Indira Gandhi on 20th August, 1979, and talked to her after an interval of 20 months. He thanked her for withdrawing Congress (I) Support to the Charan Singh Government. The mutual hatred for Janata Leaders was so great that they discovered new points of amiable contacts and co-operation with the author of the Emergency.

Charan Singh's biggest mistake, according to Madhu Limaye, was to accept Indira's treacherous support. He pathetically clutched at this straw and chose to describe it as an unconditional support.

Ambition and the consuming desire to become the Prime Minister made him blind—as it did Chandra Shekhar in 1990, when he trustfully accepted Rajiv Gandhi's support.

Ultimately Charan Singh, realising that he had lost Indira's support, resigned rather than face Lok Sabha, leading to the inevitable decision of the dissolution of the Lower House.

So the President's subjective satisfaction failed him in inviting Charan Singh to form the Government with Indira Gandhi's deceitful support. Not only this when the President refused to invite Jagjivan Ram, to form the Government, there was move to impeach the President and punish him.

After the fall of V.P. Singh's Government, the Congress Party headed by Rajiv Gandhi decided not to form the Government. And Rajiv Gandhi assured the President that his party would support Chandra Shekhar from outside for atleast a year and on no condition the support would be withdrawn before that. The President then gave consent to appoint Chandra Shekhar as the next Prime Minister. But hardly had he settled down in his seat than Rajiv Gandhi, breaking his promise, withdrew his support and brought down the Government, as his mother did in case of Charan Singh.

President R. Venkataraman was first briefed by H.K.L. Bhagat that the groups led by Devi Lal and Arun Nehru were prepared to support Rajiv Gandhi to form a Government. The President was shocked that the 'unconditional support' and oral promise of backing for atleast a year had turned out to be a sham.

The President says "I cautioned Bhagat that with all the experience of shifting loyalties, the Congress would be venturing to cross a river on a mud horse, if it relied on the alleged support of splinter groups and that the Congress should stick it out with Chandra Shekhar for some more time. I pointed out another compulsion for sticking together namely the need to pass a budget of a vote on account before the end of March failing which even salary disbursements could not be made on April, 1991."

Later, when Rajiv Gandhi came to meet him the President says, "I noticed a definite shift in Rajiv Gandhi's thinking. He was not only prepared to head the Government, but was eager to do so."

> "With all humility, I would like to record for posterity that whereas Indira Gandhi trapped Charan Singh after the fall of Morarji Desai's Government, her non-politician son, Rajiv Gandhi, not only trapped Chandra Shekhar, but also failed to behave as a gentleman with the President by not adhering to the assurance given to him that he would not withdraw his support at least for one year."

This time the subjective satisfation failed him and much against his wishes, the President had to dissolve the Parliament and ask Chandra Shekhar to be the caretaker Prime Minister till the Elections are held.

In President's own words:

> "I did not accept the resignation without feeling sorry for Chandra Shekhar . . . The office hungry coterie of the Congress Party used to misguide Rajiv Gandhi that Chandra Shekhar's attempts at building up a good image could prove deliterious to his image.
>
> *Looking back after two years, I realise my naiveness in accepting Congress Assurance of unconditional support to Chandra Shekhar. I had expected the support to last a year atleast. I realised that unequal combinations are always disadvantageous to the weaker side."*

The situation today is much worse. Atleast Ch. Charan Singh and Chandra Shekhar were the elected representatives of the People. But in case of Deve Gowda, he was neither a Member of Parliament and a representative of the people duly elected, nor was he a member of the Rajya Sabha. That is why we call him 'Prime Minister with no mandate".

Rastrapati Ji

Mr. President; you have repeated the same mistake which is of more serious nature than your earlier predecessors, by giving this country a man of no substance, Hon'ble Shri H.D. Deve Gowda to rule us by proxy. The country has indeed been robbed of their own duly elected represetative to be their Prime Minister, 'First servant' in the word of JawaharLal Nehru.

More shocking is this latest development that Deve Gowda could not retain his own seat of M.L.A. in the recent by-elections contested by his own stooge which he had vacated four months after he became the Prime Minister. It is a matter of great shame, that even after six months of his taking over as Prime Minister, he had no guts to contest for the Lok Sabha, and preferred to come from the back door by entering Rajya Sabha, and rule the countrymen as their true representative.

It is high time that suitable amendment is brought immediately making it mandatory, that the President should appoint a Prime Minister only from amongst the elected representatives of the Lok Sabha, who enjoys the transparent confidence of the majority in the House and is able to give a clean and stable government. Any splinter group which wishes to support the government must join the government and share the burden. And an elected representative from the minority party should not be allowed to head the government as was done in the case of Ch. Charan Singh, Chandra Shekhar and now Deve Gowda

Here is a flash: while the book was under print, *Statesman* carried an exciting and stimulating story under the front page caption—Gowda government in Trouble—support to be issue based and not unconditional (*Statesman* dated 17.2.1997).

Here are some excerpts

> "The Congress today decided to withdraw its unconditional support to the United Front government and made its support to governmnent issue based and conditional." The Congress Working Committee also authorised the party president, Mr. Sita Ram Kesri, to take "appropriate steps" against the government, if necessary. The Congress spokesman Mr. V.N. Gadgil said, "The CWC stand is meant to convey to the UF Leaders that our support should not be taken for granted. We are not afraid of elections."
>
> "The leaders said the resolution was not merely a lip threat' to the government. Had it been so, the CWC would not have adopted an official resolution on the matter and allowed the previous resolution of extending unconditional support to the government to continue, they said."

The Congress Party has thus followed the footsteps of Indira Gandhi qua Ch. Charan Singh, and Rajiv Gandhi qua Chandra Shekhar.

Brazenness of Legislators

*Rajinder Sachhar**

In the 50th year of independence is it not tragic that in the land of Mahatma Gandhi leaders of all the political parties should be seriously considering ways and means to remove the MPs and MLAs from the purview of the Prevention of Corruption Act? This in the face of the glorious tradition of Mahatma Gandhi who once refused to include a member in the Congress Working Committee who had apparently on the advice of a lawyer taken the usual defence in a money suit that he had not taken the money and also added in the usual lawyers jargon that even if he had taken it he was not liable to return it because it was time barred. The defence of the time-bar was found so morally reprehensible that Gandhiji refused to include him in the committee.

The contempt for public opinion and political morality has crossed all limits when the alleged justification given for this shameful exercise was that as funds have to be generated for political purposes these worthies should be freed from the fear of prosecution. This, notwithstanding that as far back as 1962 the Santhanam Committee's report on the prevention of corruption had warned that "the public belief in the prevalence of corruption at high political levels has been strengthened by the manner in which funds are collected by political parties, especially at the time of elections. Such suspicions attach not only to the ruling party but to all parties. It is, therefore, essential that the conduct of political parties should be regulated by strict principle in relation to collection of funds and electioneering."

* *Former Chief Justice, Delhi High Court*

However, nothing has been done about electoral reforms. Strangely the opposite is being suggested, namely that an ethics committee of the Members of Parliament and assemblies could be a better alternative. This suggestion would be laughable if it was not dangerously mischievous.

We have witnessed the response of the Parliament of the series of scams that have robbed the country's exchequer for even a decade starting with Bofors and recently the telecom, sugar and urea scams. In all these scams but for judicial intervention Parliament seems to have buried the scams into oblivion.

As far back as 1952 the Supreme Court had held in the Rao Shiv Bahadur Singh case that a minister was a public servant and was rightly convicted under Act.

Again in the Karunanidhi case (1979) the Supreme Court reiterated that a Chief Minister or a minister is a public servant and can be proceeded against under the Act on a sanction given by the Governor.

In a recent case (1991) of K. Veerraswamy, the Supreme Court had held that even the Chief Justices and Judges of the Supreme Court and High Court are within the purview of the Act, and sanction can be given by the President after due consideration and having regard to the opinion given by Chief Justice or the seniormost Judge, as the case may be.

In view of this, the demand of the legislators to be treated as a special class is astounding for its brazenness and in defiance of all precedent or logic. What is so special about legislators that while the highest in executive and judiciary are within the purview of the Act, this particular group of persons should be given the status of absolute monarchs irremovable and free to indulge in corruption and nepotism. I thought we had left behind the era of Henry VIII.

The excuse put forth is the so-called vagueness of judicial interpretation namely whether MPs and MLAs are public servants. If the legislators are not using this device, which is just a fig leaf, there is settled precedent easily available. I am referring to Tamil Nadu Publicmen (Criminal Misconduct) Act, 1973 which defined public man to mean any person who are or have been Chief Minister or Ministers of State or a person who is or has been member of the Legislative Assembly or Legislative Council of a State. A similar definition regarding MLAs and MPs immediately inserted in the Act, can set all controversy at rest.

Another puerile excuse is the difficulty of determining who should be the authority competent to give sanction. This is on the ground that MLAs and MPs being elected cannot be removed by any authority. But this argument proceeds on the basis of retention of Section 6(1) (c) of the Act, as at present, which requires the sanction of the authority competent to remove a public servant. Now if the legislators were not taking cover behind this technicality all that needs to be done is to add a separate clause in the Act that in the case of MPs and MLAs, the sanctioning authority will be the President or the Governor, just as in the case of the Prime Minister, the Chief Justice of India or a Chief Minister.

The Supreme Court has already ruled that it is not necessary that the authority competent to give sanction for prosecution or the authority competent to remove the public servant should be vertically superior in the hierarchy in which the office of the public servant exists. There is no such requirement under Section 6. The power to give sanction for prosecution can be conferred on any authority. As a matter of fact under the British Prevention of Corruption Act, 1906 the power to give consent for prosecution for an offence under the Act has been conferred upon the Attorney-General or Solicitor-General.

Indeed there is already much outcry about this provision for obtaining sanction in the case of public servants. Critics complain that it is used to protect corrupt favourites by the politicians.

In my view, instead of trying to seek exemption from the purview of the Act, MLAs and MPs would be enhancing their stature if they were to take the stand that they are willing to trust impartial investigating agency for initiating prosecution if there is credible material to do so, and that they do not require the protection of any previous sanction by any authority.

If the reason claimed for exemption of the MPs and MLAs from being prosecuted under the Act was that a grave situation would arise, it must be pointed out that while the abetter, that is a bribe giver to the legislator, could be found guilty under Section 165-A of the Indian Penal Code and convicted, the main culprit (the legislator) would escape because he would not be covered within the purview of the Act. In a civilised society the law cannot be assumed to be leading to such a disturbing result, to use the language of the Supreme Court.

The immediacy with which the Government, the MPs and MLAs quash this controversy by publicly repudiating any such intention will be the measure of their bona fide of a public declaration in the equality of all before the law and in the democratic tradition of the Constitution. Otherwise it may be said that though our Constitution grants equality to all its citizens, in reality the legislators are a class by themselves and are more equal than others. Such an approach would be destructive of the basic structure of our Constitution.

Open letter to the President — By Rajinder Puri

Dear Mr President,

The matter I wish to raise is so important that it deserves public transparency. Therefore I am writing this open letter.

You cannot be unaware of the grave public disquiet caused by the steady deterioration in our national politics. Senior leaders now even talk of changing the system.

But no system can succeed unless those implementing it have integrity. Today no political leader or group has sufficient moral authority to obtain public approval for introducing systematic change.

There is no constitutional provision for a new Constituent Assembly. The law precludes change in the basic structure of our Constitution. We are constrained therefore to introduce change with continuity. And we must remain within our basic Constitution.

Mr President, you are elected by both Houses of Parliament and all the Assemblies and legislatures in the country. You have the widest mandate. You are the Supreme Defender of the Constitution and supreme commander of our defence forces.

As the appointer of all executive posts in the Government, and the final signatory for converting Bill into law, you bear the ultimate responsibility for protecting the Republic.

Today our Republic faces grave danger.

It is axiomatic that beyond a stage quantitative change becomes a qualitative change. Corruption in high places is now so widespread that our system of governance is virtually destroyed.

Leaders cutting across party lines have condemned judicial activism for this malaise. The Prime Minister himself made disparaging remarks about public interest litigations.

What are we to understand? Should citizens not point out cases of corruption when public interest is damaged? Should courts not admit cases where prima facie evidence justifies investigation? Should official investigative agencies not probe politicians as they do ordinary citizens who transgress the law?

Senior national leaders, including former Prime Ministers and the present Prime Minister, have jointly decided to amend the law and exclude MPs from purview of the Prevention of Corruption Act. It is proposed that MPs will not qualify as public servants.

After the current session of Parliament ends this week, the Government plans to present an Ordinance to this effect for you to sign.

There is no law at present which empowers the Election Commission to question political parties about their sources of revenue. Nor can it monitor the expenditure of individual politicians. All money received by MPs regardless of whether it is spent for the party or for personal use will therefore be immune from legal scrutiny once MPs cease to be public servants.

The proposed move by politicians to circumvent prosecution exposes their hollow claims. Those accused of corruption refuted the charges against them as false. Then why do they not prove their innocence in court? Instead they want to change the law!

This attempt by politicians to amend the law for evading prosecution is brazen.

By this Ordinance the politicians will declare war against the people.

The people will fight back.

The question is, Mr President: Will you support the Government or justice?

Will you fight for the politicians or for the people?

Will you sign the Ordinance or return it?

Mr President, I am confident that you will not let the people down. You will not sign the Ordinance. You will intervene in the manner you think best to save the Republic.

In this dark hour the people of India can only turn to you.

Courtesy: *Statesman,* 18.12.1996

Betrayal

*Avtar Singh Sohal**

When Wilt Thou save the people?
O God of mercy; When?
The people, Lord; The people
Not thrones and crowns but
men;
God save the people; Thine
They are;
Thy children, as thy angels
fair;
Save them from bondage and
despair;
God save the people;

Ebenezer Elliot

(2) The unprivileged, down trodden and propertyless masses did not possess suffrage qualifications and were thus excluded from participation in the work of framing Constitution of India. However our wisemen whom the task of composing the instrument of governance was entrusted introduced myth when they prefaced it with the much orchestrated rhetorical exaggeration that "we the people" of India . . . . "

(3) Have we ever seriously introspected as to whether our constitution has responded to the aspirations of the teeming millions who were not represented in the constituent assembly?

---

* Advocate, Supreme Court of India

My head spins, my imagination is whacked, my mind is excruciatingly anguished and my nerves get benumbed when I perceive all pervading indifference, inertia, complacence as if the entire nation is under epilectic seizure.

The nation is not stirred at all over appalling moribund and outrageously denigrative and subversive state of affairs.

4) We are on the threshold of a new millennuim and have already traversed half a century as a free nation. A vibrant, pulsating and robust nation cannot afford stagnation, inaction, list-lessness or slovenness. These are cancerous maladies which if not purged off soon would mercilessly eat up the very vitals of our polity. I often shudder when I see that the vitals of our body politic have virtually been eaten up and we are fastly marching towards terminal stage.

(5) Five decades have been allowed to be frittered away by us. We are still a developing nation. Some other countries who embarked upon the task of restructuring and developing themselves contemporaneously or much later than us have entered into galaxy of the developed and most developed nations leaving us trailing behind and gasping for breath. It is lamentable to think that the pace at which we are marching we are sure to continue trailing behind others in the foreseable future. Our future looks obscure, uncertain and woefully disastrous.

(6) There appears to be no noticeable, perceptible or meaningful debate, introspection or serious inquiry into myriad causes which have slowed or retarded our progression. The only hackneyed excuse shamefacedly is being pleaded by our political class is the proliferation of population. Though we are over populated yet it is not such unsurmountable problem which should be allowed to impede our progress. In fact it is only an alibi being used by the political class to cover up themselves for their failures, incompetence, lack of vision and direction. We have become self sufficient in food which is our basic necessity. In sum explosion of the population is not the main cause for our failures. We must address overselves the real causes which have impeded and retarded our onward march towards prosperity. We must identify the reasons which have kept our teeming millions below the poverty line whose existence is not better than of chattels.

Why have we not even been able to provide potable water to 90% of our people, much less education, providing shelter, nutritious diet to their children and hygenic and healthy environment and conditions worthy of a human being? Why the benefits of the freedom have not percolated to the grass roots? There is a lengthy catalogue of similar nagging questions which are crying and begging for answers from the persons who matter in the present dispensation and who are responsible for pushing the nation to this pass.

(7) My outpourings may be dismissed as melancholic and pessimistic expression but if the socio-economic and political milieu obtaining today is forensically analysed only a naive, unaffected and a simplton person would disagree with my feelings of dejection, disenchantment and depression.

(8) My mind is severly pierced with agony when I feel that goodness, righteousness, probity and rectitude from public life have taken wings and flown into the dark night of falsehood, degradation and depravity. I espy not any ray of hope and I desperately grope for the proverbial silver lining and feel like crying as to where is the path of redemption.

(9) Where that stuff has disappeared which provided fodder to the cannons of freedom movement? Have we become bereft of dedicated, devoted, austere, righteous, selfless and fiercely nationalists who would sacrifice and offer anything at the alter of the nation?

(10) For Fifty years we have been feigning to practise democracy and what is the outcome of so called democratic churning? Absolute corruption, predatory, treachery, third class criminalised political class with not perception or vision, denigration of moral values sectarianism parochialism and downgraded anti people administrative structure. The worst outcome is the inefficient, insensitive non compos, unprincipled and pervert leadership.

(11) Our electorates are among the maturest in the world but it is very distressing the leadership which we have thrown up is not worthy and capable of providing matching stewardship to the people. The political class who destined to preside over the fate and fortune of the teeming millions cannot be characterized true representatives of the people. The electoral system prevailing in our country is so stringent and complex

which does not permit sincere, rightful and meaningful person having no material resources and muscle power to aspire to be an elected representative. The lower strata of our society often remains unrepresented. Though unprivileged people nolens volens exercise their valuable right of franchise, yet, their ballots are often usurped by someone who imposes himself on them on the strength of money, material resources, political clout and muscle power which is not in dearth for those who themselves have criminal background. Service of the people is not their credo instead self aggrandizement is their guiding motive.

(12) We have adopted West Minister system of parliamentary democracy but our political class adnauseam attributes all ills to the system itself instead of acknowledging the reality that it is this class alone which has not only atrophied the system but also frustrated the aspirations of the teeming millions. What type of these elected representatives, political bosses are who need protective security umbrella at the cost of their own Constituents whom they claim to represent and serve. Is it not gross travestry and irony of fate, and the circumstances that those who vow to serve people are scared of them and need security from them?

(13) Let us advert to state of present governance. A conglermenation of 13 divergent political outfits has usurped the reins of power. Thirteen pebbles do not make a mountain. The Constituents of this so called United Front (which is woefully ununited) have nothing common among themselves excepting greed to weild power. Vociferously they claim to have acquired mandate to rule. It is prepostrous to say that mandate is for coalition. In fact the electorates rejected all the political outfits and administered clear and unambiguous warning that they would not allow anyone to take them for ride. Conversely speaking the electorate wands political class to evolve two party system if the Westminister System has to be retained as multi party system is not conducive for Parliamentary form of Government. Every constituent of the United Front went to poll on the strength of its own manifesto. For the sake of usruping power 13 constituents said goodbye to their respective manifestos, and devised Common Minimum Programme. Is it not fraud committed

on the electorate? It is sad that the present ruling class has no mandate to rule and especially the Prime Minister, the Chief Executive of the country. My esteemed friend Dr. Janak Raj Jai has highlighted the legal and other facets to substantiate that incumbent P.M. has no legitimate right to head the country. He has done Yeoman's service to the nation by challenging the appointment of Prime Minister. I too have lot to say on this aspect but I refrain it from doing so as Dr. Jai has taken care of those vital points which I want to comment upon. However, it would suffice to add that the political bankruptcy reached nadir point when the circumstances and exigencies threw up and catapulted person like Gowda as head of the State. He was member of Lok Sabha elected on Janata Ticket, when Narasimha Rao was struggling hard to muster majority in the House, Mr. Gowda wanted to jump into the band-wagon of Rao for obvious reasons of quid pro quo. He was dissuaded by friends and by a very prominent astrologer Mr. P.K. Bhanot that such step would tantamount to committing political harakari. My astrologer friend in my presence at my residence very forcefully and persuasively brought home to Gowda that he would be the next chief Minister of Karnataka and advised him to stay put which he faithfully did. However, he absented himself from the house when the house debated confidence motion.

(14) He is man of very ordinary intelligence possessing prejudices, fads and shortcomings which an ordinary mortal being would possess. Even after acquiring a celebrity status he has not extricated himself from narrow mindedness, personal vendetta and weaknesses. Is it not shameful that our Prime Minister needs judicial intervention to silence and stifle his personal criticism ?

(15) I am reminded of the times more than five hundred years back when Babar invaded and captured India. He established despotic rule. At that time there was one highly enlightened soul who challenged the despot by calling him as butcher and his minions as dogs. Guru Nanak had fearlessly condemned the then prevailing oppressive dispensation.

(16) Today we have democracy but voice of dissent is often stifled and silenced by coercive means. When posterity will learn

that the Prime Minister of India sought judicial protection to silence his criticism they would not pardon us particularly the intelligentia as to why voice of disapproval was not roused.

(17) We the people of India, the ultimate sovereigns should no more countenance to the antics, tantrums malfeasance of anti people downgraded political class maladminstring and malfunctioning of our corrupt and ailing bureaucracy and set ourselves on the path of establishing Ram Rajya.

(18) In theory we have democracy but in practice our government is oligarchy. Here people rule by reasons of wealth, physical prowess and manipulations and poor are covertly and overtly excluded from participation in the actual governance. Ruling cliques have acquired unlimited powers which have corroded their conscience, hardened their hearts and confounded their understanding.

We need a political messiah today with vision, perception, moral strength and authority, deep concern at heart for the poor who can stand with them, alleviate their untold miseries inflicted upon them by anti people dispensation, and extricate them from shackless of oppressive brute force of the political class; a benevolvent guide, philosopher and friend of the poor who can fight against injustice, inequilities, oppression, deprivations and tribulations. People are ready for another revolution, this time not against colonial rulers but against our own unkind, fossilised political class.

Let us supplicate to the divine power, the Lord Almighty to give us strength to guard ourselves and fight against the privileged class who on the pretext of trusteeship and service have pillaged us by their greedy cupidity.

Let us shake and shed our slumber, despondancy and inertia organise ourselves as one man to fight for equal opportunities, fair deal and empancipation and establish a civilised society with pristine glory where everyone lives with dignity and honour.

No more dithering my countrymen, rise.

Judicial Propriety and President's Shortsightedness

Democracy is a means to achieve a true democratic voter, a relevance whereof is known only to the elections and their results. In every country wedded to secularism, rule of law and democracy, elections have become a necessity and is a part of our convention. Highlighting on the system of the illrooted democracy, partly received in bounty by the British system and partly through the power of election generating into corruption which is manifested in various ways, a democratic individual has started having apprehensions about the fate of the future democratic country like sovereign of India.

History often repeats but we never try to learn therefrom. Isms and various political parties have their own merits and demerits. The end result is consequence which was witnessed by me not only as student of politics but also as a responsible person for upholding the rule of law and the Constitution which we are expounding. The results of Indian Parliament elections were declared in the year 1996 sometime in the month of May, and as luck would have it, no party could gain absolute majority. BJP was the largest single party having secured around 190 M.P.s, Congress with 140 and various regional parties around 178 seates.

The President of India, Dr. Shanker Dayal Sharma, requested the Leader of BJP to form the Government and secure the vote of confidence on the floor of the House. Shri Atal Behari Vajpai was sworn as Prime Minister on 14th May, 1996. He could not muster enough majority to win confidence vote on 27th May in the Parliament and thus gracefully resigned as Prime Minister, the same day i.e. on 27th May, 1996.

All Political parties started hob-nobbing and various unscrupless Politicians started pressurizing the President. I have already disclosed various facts in the earlier Chapter titled "Untold Story".

Shri. H.D. Deve Gowda, the then Chief Minister of Karnataka although branded as king of corruption by an economist and one time aspirant to the post of Vice-Chancellor of Karnataka University, however, became the new Prime Minister to the utter dismay of the Indian electorate. He was chosen by few, rejected by majority yet there being no conscience, his name rolled-over against all and I believe it was a sheer luck.

Compelled by the circumstances and in the interest of the nation, I had to challenge his appointment through a Writ Petition bearing No. 2408/1996 before the High Court of Delhi at New Delhi. The Hon'ble two Judges of the High Court (Mr. Justice Jaspal Singh and Mr. Justice J.K. Mehra) however, dismissed the writ petition on the 5th July, 1996 upholding the appointment of Shri H.D. Deve Gowda as Prime Minister. Although I gave enough material to bring home my point, besides quoting constitutional experts like Mr. H.M. Seervai, Dr. B.R. Ambedkar and the Constituent Assembly Debate, yet the Court upheld the appointment of Deve Gowda as the Prime Minister.

After the Judgement I had many sleepless nights but keeping a hope against hope I decided to challenge the said Judgement before the Hon'ble Supreme Court of India. My friends, well-wishers and public spirited people advised me not to appear in-person but to present it through an Advocate who is well versed in constitution and the rule of law. After giving my careful thought I contacted my old time friend and constitutional exponent Arvind Kumar and he took his own time in making his decision to challenge the Judgement. In such circumstances S.L.P. was filed through his own wife Mrs. Laxmi Arvind (Advocate-on-Record) in the Supreme Court of India challenging the Judgement and Order of the High Court dt. 5.7.1996. The said petition was numbered as S.L.P. (Civil) N. 19606/1996 after long persuasion.

After filing this petition and immediately after it being numbered, a news appeared in *Rashtriya Sahara* of 28th September, 1996, under the caption "*Aakhir Deve Gowda Raat mein Mukhya Nyaadhish se Milne Kyon Gaye?"* (Why Deve Gowda went to see the Chief Justice of India at the mid of the night?)

I was perplexed and at that time one more petition under Article-32 of the Constitution of India was pending in the Hon'ble Supreme Court of India challenging the appointment of Mr. H.D. Deve Gowda as Prime Minister. Sensing that the judiciary may not be blamed tomorrow, I under judicial discipline immediately informed the Hon'ble Chief Justice of India vide my letter dt. 28th September, 1996 that his Lordship Hon'ble Chief Justice of India may refer both the petitions to a larger bench so that the issues raised in these petitions be finally decided by the Highest Court of land. I had also informed in writing that my petition was also pending in the Supreme Court. This letter was personally handed over to the P.P.S. of Hon'ble Chief Justice of India.

I never expected that the Hon'ble Chief Justice of India would not take the letter in its right spirit. As a student of the faculty of the judicial discipline, I must say that where the Judgement is in direct challenge before any court, it would be against judicial propriety if the said Judgement is considered and approved in colateral proceedings. It was unfortunate that the Hon'ble Chief Justice met the Prime Minister against whom the petitions were pending in the Supreme Court of India and the propriety demanded, as a word of caution what Hon'ble Mr. Justice P.K. Goswami of the Supreme Court of India quoted with an approval, that such meetings ought to be avoided. Without entering into the said controversy which is looming large, I would venture say that the Hon'ble Chief Justice may have refrained from pronouncing Judgement on 6th November, 1996. My petition was kept in abeyance and was only listed after the Judgement being pronounced in S.P. Anand's Case on 26th November, 1996. Mr. Arvind Kumar, aided with other counsels being instructed on my behalf appeared before the Supreme Court of India and urged that 'the Judgement of the Delhi High Court is not constitutionally correct yet it was pleaded by him that he may be allowed to urge two more facts viz. Mr. H.D. Deve Gowda continuing as a member of Karnataka Assembly and his entering into the parliament through backdoor i.e. Rajya Sabha.' It was also stated by Mr. Arvind Kumar that a review was filed in the High Court which was dismissed by the Division bench of the

High Court on 21.11.1996. He however, submitted that irrespective of the Judgement in review he ought to be heard on additional grounds and facts in view of the provisions of Order-8, Rule-8 C.P.C., yet the Hon'ble Court directed him to file the copy of the Judgement in review petition, and the matter was accordingly adjourned.

This matter finally came up before the Chief Justice's Bench on 24.01.1997 when the petition was sought to be argued by Mr. Arvind Kumar and he also circulated his legal submissions. It was urged by Mr. Arvind Kumar that the views quoted of Dr. Ambedkar do not relate to the appointment of the Prime Minister and before he could make his own submissions and refer to the books and authorities, the Court told him that "we will pass appropriate Orders." Legal Submissions raised in this case are mentioned hereunder :

(1) That the President of India has a Constitutional power and sanction to appoint the Prime Minister of India. The Powers are uncontrolled, without any guidelines yet coupled by Oath as prescribed in Article-51(a), 53, 61, 74 and 75, 85 and 361 of the Constitution of India, it is crystal clear that though the powers and discretion are unwritten and undefined, yet the President of India is guided by certain Constitutional mandate, Constitutional conventions and the preamble of the Constitution of India. The President is not under the control and command of the Prime Minister or his Council of Ministers, irrespective of the fact that the word 'shall' has been introduced under Article.74(1), by the Constitution 42nd Amendment Act of 1976. The President is bound to appoint the Prime Minister keeping in view the intentions of the framers of the Constitution for the purposes of collective responsibility in the Lok Sabha and for the stability of the Country in a democratic manner. Without challenging the validity of the said amendment it is submitted that the President has some residuary powers in his Constitutional discretion.

(2) That the appointment of the Prime Minister of India has to be traced into the practice and tradition based on British Model and as per Law laid down by this Hon'ble Court in various rulings including those reported in AIR 1974 SC 2192 and AIR 1971 SC 1002, and lastly on the Provisions of the Constitution. Tested on touch stone of these Principles, it will be apparent that the Prime Minister must be an elected member

and the Leader of Lok Sabha, he must enjoy the confidence of the Lok Sabha and that such a person has to be above board without any insinuation whatsoever. The President of India in choosing such a person is further guided by his Oath which is absolutely different from all other Oaths administered to the other Constitutional functionaries and while making such appointment the President of India has to keep in mind the justification of the service and the well being of the people of India besides the President as a first citizen, has to cherish and follow the noble ideals and to uphold and protect the unity and integrity of India. Mr. R. Venkataraman, the Former President of India in his book 'My Presidential years' has clearly mentioned that he committed a mistake by appointing Shri Chandra Shekher as a Prime Minister of India having no majority with him on the assurance of support by the Congress Party headed by Shri Rajiv Gandhi. President has to act in good faith. President has the authority to appoint but does not have the power of Constitutional will to remove him.

(3) With great respect it is submitted that the 'Prime Minister' is not included in the word 'Minister' as used in Article 75(5) of the Constitution of India. It is submitted that the Constitution of India prescribes a marked distinction between the Prime Minister and the Council of Ministers. Further the Council of Ministers may have the Minister of Cabinet rank and other Ministers. To be very specific as per our Constitution, there is marked distinction between a Prime Minister, a Minister of Cabinet rank and other Ministers. Articles-74, 75, 77, 78, and 352 of the Constitution of India have to be read in reaching to the aforesaid conclusion. A Prime Minister cannot be equated either with the Council of Ministers, or with Ministers of Cabinet rank or otherwise. Needless to mention that Prime Minister has unfettered and uncontrolled authority of forming a Council of Ministers by making an appointment and has also the powers to dismiss or seek resignation of any member of Council of Ministers. Prime Minister is not under any Constitutional command to appoint any Ministers. He may run the Government on his own. Similarly no condition can be attached to the appointment of a Prime Minister by the President of India. Assuming without admitting that Article-75(5) includes a Prime Minister, it would mean that for one reason or the other if the

Prime Minister does not get elected within six months the whole Government falls but in case of a Minister it does not happen so. The framers of the Constitution of India also did not mean and include Prime Minister into the Provisions of Arrticle 75(5) as will be apparent in the reply and debate of Dr. B.R. Ambedkar in respect of the Amendment No. 1322 and 1326 in the Constituent Assembly on 31st December, 1948. The total sum and substance of the Debates are that Article 75(5) of the Constitution of India does not include Prime Minister but a Minister alone. Petitioner further ventures to say that even in the appointment of a minister of a cabinet rank Article-75(5) ought not be applicable and ought to be excluded. In giving this interpretation we will harmonize various Provisions of the Constitution including those of emergency. Article-78 further clearly gives a distinction between a Minister and a Prime Minister and as a matter of fact the Prime Minister is an important link between the President and the Executive. Further the Constitution ought not be read in its literal sense but must be interpreted as per changing circumstances. Assuming without admitting, President has the arbitrary powers to appoint Prime Minister, reading without in between the lines, with qualifications of Article-75(5), it will be apparent that any one could be appointed Prime Minister to the subjective satisfaction of the President of India and thus the two Constitutional functionaries may destroy and abuse of the Provision of the Constitution of India including emergency and if it is propounded further it will appear that such two functionaries having hands in gloves together may destroy the sovereignty of the nation by repealing the Constitution and doing whatever they wish to, may be at the cost of civil revolution. The Constitution must, therefore, be interpreted in the manner it has been interpreted in Keshvanand Bharti's Case, Chief Justice's Appointment Case and Kihota Hollohon Cases.

(4) The appointment of the Prime Minister ought not be read literally to appoint a Minister but it is the formation of the Union Government, which controls the functioning of all the States. Further as held in U.N. Rao's Case (AIR 1971 SC 1002) that the Office of the Prime Minister and institution of the Council of ministers continues to function even during dissolution of the house and the collective responsibility as envisaged under Article-

75(3) must therefore, be read with exception 'except when the House of People stands dissolved or prorogued'. The appointment, therefore, has to be more critically tested on the touch stone of the democracy as per preamble of the Constitution. The judgments of this Hon'ble Court in the matter of Shri H.S. Verma need not detain us as there are qualitative differences between the Office of the Prime Minister and that of the Chief Minister.

(5) As per Constitutional mandate, conventions and practice till this day in India as well as in Britain, it is absurd to think that a member of the State Legislative Assembly continues to govern this Country having secured an appointment to the post of Prime Minister. It is ridiculous even in democratic thinking. Our Constitution has categorically introduced in the negative form that no person should be member of Parliament and the Legislative Assembly of States. It is submitted that no sooner a person claims an appointment within the Provisions of Article-75(5), and moreover that of a Prime Minister it becomes abundantly clear that he in order to give stable Government, has the willingness, desire, capability and suitability to contest the election of the Parliament, and therefore he immediately comes within the ambit of Article-101(2). Hence it is submitted that no sooner he takes an Oath of a Minister in a Union Government, he must resign his seat from the member of the legislative Assembly immediately as otherwise his willingness and desire of becoming the member of Parliament comes under cloud vitiating his Oath and Ministership. It is further submitted that unless he resigns his seat previously or as per Provision of Article-101(2) of the Constitution or immediately after taking the Oath as prescribed in Article-75(4), he should be deemed to have vacated and/or abandoned premises submitted that Shri H.D. Deve Gowda while taking Oath under Article-74(4) and accepting the mandate of Article 75(5) of the Constitution, was already a member of Karnataka legislative Assembly and his Oath is violated since he did not resign from the said seat in the State Legislative Assembly. Even assuming that he could legally continue to occupy the two positions that of Prime Minister and member of Karnataka Legislative Assembly (which is a fraud and absurdity on the face of the Constitutional Provisions besides an abuse of the Constitutional belief, sanction and powers), he

ought to have resigned his seat in legislature of the Karnataka Assembly on or before 31st of July, 1996 as per Provisions of Article-101(2) and as per rules made by the president in this regard. Having failed thus, his continuation on the post of Prime Minister is vitiated and that he has no moral, Constitutional and democratic right to act as the Prime Minister of India. He is thus abusing the Office of the Prime Minister w.e.f. 1.6.1996 without any legal and Constitutional sanctity.

(6) That the Constitutional requirement for a Prime Minister as per conventions and practice till today in India is that the Prime Minister must get elected to the House of People through direct elections besides being the Leader of the said house.

Shri Deve Gowda has failed to get elected to the Lok Sabha within a period of six months from the date of his appointment and as such Shri Deve Gowda is not entitled to act as a Prime Minister of the Country w.e.f. December 1, 1996. This is on the assumption that he is entitled to get his appointment subject to Article-75(5) of the Constitution of India. H.D. Deve Gowda has entered into the Parliament through back door i.e. in the Rajya Sabha. This is against the Constitutional norms, conventions and practice. It is fraud on the Constitution that a member of Rajya Sabha may advise the President, who in his turn is bound for the dissolution of House where he does not have any control and/or vote. Besides the Prime Minister of the Country is expected to keep himself above board and is further expected to honour the Constitutional mandate and duties as enshrined in Article-51(a) of the Constitution of India being an important Citizen and the head of the Executive. The framers of the Constitution of India never visualized that the office of the Prime Ministership shall be held by such a person who in order to secure his seat as such will enter in Rajya Sabha and thereby commit Constitutional impropriety and would be ruling the Country by the mischief of proxy.

(7) In democratic system to which our Constitution is wedded, the Principle of direct election is not only the rule of democratic law but also it has acquired the status of convention and our Country has followed this convention till today.

The interpretation of the Constitution as given in this case of S.P. Anand by His Lordship Hon'ble Chief Justice of India reflects his views which were held in minority in the Judge's

Case pronounced by the 9 Judges Constitution Bench reported in AIR 1994 SC 268 AT Page 367. Besides these judicial facts and views, the Hon'ble Court ought to have considered the appointment in its real perspective and whether such appointments are within the frame work of democracy and the Constitution which we are expounding.

Needless to mention that the Constitutional expert Mr. H.M. Seervai has categorically held that the appointment of Shri Charan Singh on the prerogative of the President was absolutely uncalled for besides factually and constitutionally wrong. Similar appointments of Shri V.P. Singh and Chandra Shekher have also yielded no fruitful result in preserving either democracy or Constitution. I am afraid such appointments are against the Constitutional integrity and are the negation of the Sovereign Democratic Republic.

Hard to believe yet the facts remain that due to such inherent lack of constitutional will, indiscipline and power, the criminals and un-scrupulous people have made their inroads into the politics and now I feel ashamed when I find that political parties are crowded by such type of persons. Criminalisation of politics is not the end, it's just the beginning. We all must safeguard our democracy.

Mr. H.M. Seervai in his treatise constitutional law of India Third Edition in its Volume-2 Epilogue from page 2706 to 2728 has categorically discussed the Defection, the fall of Janata Government and the President's powers. He has categorically held that the President's action in 1979 was clearly contrary to Article-75(1) read with Article-75(3) and the convention which is necessary employed in that article on the question of accepting the resignation of Mr. Morarji Desai and his Council of Ministers and further asking him to continue till arrangements were made. He has further stated 'as far as can be judged from published accounts, there is no evidence that the President realized that it was not enough that this or that person could form a Ministry commanding a temporary majority.' He has further quoted with approval 'it was necessary for the President to obtain in writing that those persons would give general support to one or the other leader for a reasonable period of time to carry on the Government. Had he obtained such writing and the persons failed to act according to their written promise, the President would have been absolved from blame, and the public in first instance and the electors in the last, would have dealt with those who had broken their promise.'

Seervai's warnings were fruitless exercise yet the President of India again committed same historical blunder and realized so vide illustration of Mr. R. Venkataraman when he admits his naivness (in his book *'My Presidential Years'*), admitting that he had committed mistake by appointing Shri Chandra Shekher as a Prime Minister of India having no majority with him on the so-called assurances and support by the Congress Party headed by Shri Rajiv Gandhi.

Alas, the President had gone through the views expressed by Seervai in his book Constitutional Law of India, Vol.II, wherein he had thoroughly discussed the fate of the minority governments, with particular reference to Charan Singh's Government. Not only this the country would have been saved from such unscruplous Prime Minister, who not even was stranger (being neither a member of Lok Sabha nor Rajya Sabha) but also was in hopeless minority, outwardly supported by the so called United Front which was created after the election, out of compulsion in order to keep BJP out of race, by fair or foul means.

President R. Venkataraman's following statement (My Presidential Years—1982) would also have served as a good guide.

> "I did not accept the resignation without feeling sorry for Chandra Shekhar. During his few months in office, he had handled Parliament competently and was responsive to suggestions from the pressure of the Congress Party, which I am afraid, assumed that it was `the real government, and Chandra Shekhar only a proxy. The office hungry coterie of Congress Party used to misguide Rajiv Gandhi that Chandra Shekhar's attempts at building up a good image could prove deleterious to his image. Looking back after two years, I realise my naiveness in accepting the Congress assurance of "unconditional support" to Chandra Shekhar. I realised that unequal combinations are always disadvantageous to the weaker side."

Parting note: In all fairness, keeping in view that justice is not only done, but it must be seen to have been done, the Hon'ble Chief Justice of India could have excluded his name from the Bench hearing my special Leave Petition. Having decided to sit on the Bench alongwith Sujata Manohar and G.B. Patnaik the other two illustrious Judges, full opportunity should have been afforded to my counsel, Arvind Kumar, a constitutional lawyer of more than 30 years standing at the Bar.

In S.P. Anand's case (1996) 6 SCC 734) the Hon'ble Chief Justice of India is on record to say: para 18 (Page 745):

Before we part, we cannot help mentioning that on the issues on the constitutional law, litigants who can lay no claim to have no expert knowledge in that field should refrain from filing petition, which if we may say so, are often drafted in a casual and cavaliar fashion giving an extempore appearance not having had a second look. This is the impression that one gets on reading the present petition. It is of utmost importance that those who invoke this court's jurisdiction seeking a waiver of the locus standi rule must exercise restraint in moving the courts by not plunging in areas, wherein they are not well versed . . . . He must remember that as a person seeking to espouse a public cause, he must owe it to the public as well as to the court that he does not rush to court without undertaking a research, even if he is qualified or competent to raise the issue . . . ."

My petition was filed on 13.9.96 and judgement in S.P. Anand's Case was delivered on 7.11.96. If our petition had been heard before pronouncement of judgement in S.P. Anand's Case, the Hon'ble Supreme Court would have got the assistance of a Senior member of the Bar and would have handed over to the country the verdict of the highest court on issues of great public importance which have been begging for a final decision since a long time. Later on, with dogged persuation we were able to have our SLP listed, which was ultimately heard on 24.1.1997. My counsel spent many sleepless nights preparing this case so that he was able to assist the Court in as best manner as possible. Not only this he was ready with legal submissions in writing which had been filed on the day of hearing.

Our review petition in High Court was not dismissed on merits, but only on maintainability, as the Learned Attorney General of India, Ashok Desai, did not want to argue on merits.

Unfortunately, the Supreme Court on the date of hearing perhaps was in a different mood, and by not permitting my Counsel to argue in full length, deprived themselves from the assistance available to them in order to give a reasonable judgement on the various issues raised by us in the SLP.

Finding himself helpless, my Counsel prayed, "Your Lordships are omnipotent and can invoke Art 142, to do complete justice and can decide the issue raised by us, even though technically they can't be heard. The Court smilingly observed. "It is our discretion and we are not inclined to use that discretion in this case." The net result is that my countrymen have been deprived of a final verdict on the vital issues of great public importance raised by us in the petition before the highest Court. The only way left for an humble citizen like me, is perhaps to go to the people's Court for a suitable amendment in the laws that only an elected representative from the Lok Sabha should be able to adorn the office of the Prime Minister.

On judicial propriety I venture to reproduce below para 172, of the Supreme Court judgement delivered by Justice P.K. Goswami (State of Rajasthan vs. Union of India—AIR 1977 S.C. 1917).

"172. I part with the records with a cold shudder.

The Chief Justice was good enough to tell us that acting President saw him during the time we were considering judgement after having already announced the order that there was mention of the pending matter during the conversation. I have given this relation the most anxious thought and even the strongest judicial restraint which a judge would prefer to exercise, leaves me no option, but to place this on record hoping that the majesty of the high office of the President, who should be beyond the high watermark, of any controversy, suffers not in justice."

Six Months on, What's the Grade?

Mulayam Singh Yadav (Defence)

Quick to clinch Sukhoi deal

Defence experts are happy that Mulayam's ministry — though it seems to flounder on other fronts — was reasonably quick to clinch the deal with Russia for the acquisition of two squadrons of Sukhoi — 30 MK, arguably the next century's multi role premier combat aircraft. Former chief of the IAF, N.C. Suri says that the fact that the deal fructified under the present government, even though the spade work might have been done by the earlier government, must go to the raksha mantri's credit.

Rapport with the forces

Lieutenant General Satish Nambiar, Director, United Services Institution, the defence services' think tank, adds, "His readiness to speak up for defence requirements is commendable. Coming from a rural background, he is able to strike a chord with the lower echelons within the defence forces the bulk of which comes from rural India."

Unnecessary delays and adhocism: "The bitter truth" says retired Rear Admiral Satyindra Singh "is that despite Yadav's cliched assertions that all legitimate defence requirements will be met, national security continues to be dealt with in an utterly ad hoc and lackadaisical manner." For one, files that are to be passed by Mulayam, have to be transalated into Hindi which doubles the paper work and leads to unnecessary delays.

Not serious about portfolio

Experts point out that instead of making futuristic plans and equipping the forces with men and material to cope with the emerging threats, even their urgent requirements are not met. As Singh puts it, "With a non-residential raksha mantri who is more interested in the Samajwadi party's struggle in UP than the curcial issue of national defence, one can hardly expect better." The general feeling among experts is that is that the defence minister has yet to learn to take national defence with the seriousness it deserves.

(Panelist: Satish Nambiar and Satyindra Singh, defence analysts)

P. Chidambaram (Finance)

A sense of continuity and the desire to get on with reforms: Chidambaram has been seen as the sole voice of fiscal prudence in the government. Apprehensions that the government will disintegrate have been put to rest by him. "Industry's wariness about the government is clearly due to the non-protectionist attitude towards business." says Swaminathan Anklesaria Aiyar.

Good understanding of liberalisation: "Whereas liberalisation was limited to delicensing, converting quotas into tariffs and cutting taxes in the Congress regime, Chidambaram clearly sees the government as a facilitator, and not as provider. This was reflected in his first budget," says Subhashish Gangopadhyay.

A brave front : Experts feel the FM's performance has to be seen in the light of the previous government's policies, as many hard decisions, including monitoring of administered prices have been passed on. "Under so many forces, within and without, he is doing a reasonably good job," says B.B. Bhattacharya.

Conflicting signals

"The government's dilemma seems to be — how much growth should be sacrified to achieve social justice. But the FM cannot be blamed, as the confusion seems to be arising out of the contradictory perceptions of development amongst different constituents of the UF," says Bhattacharya. He adds: "The fall in foreign direct investment is also because of this. While the PM and FM want to welcome foreign investors in general, some others, like the I&B minister, have not been encouraging."

High on intent, low on execution

"Chidambaram could have pushed through hard decisions like disinvestment of PSUs and opening up of financial markets as it would take politics to resolve them. But he has failed," says Gangopadhyay. "The Expenditure Commission, which was supposed to have submitted its report by December, is nowhere near it," says Aiyar.

Slow to react

"The current trend of recession has followed a very tight monitory policy pursued by the previous government on the eve of the last general elections. The current government took a little time in setting it correct," says Bhattacharya. Moreover, he adds, decisions announced in the new credit policy could have come outside of it, so that their effects could be realised better.

(Panelists: B.B. Bhattacharya, professor, IEG; Subhashish Gangopadhyay, ISI; Swaminathan Anklesria Aiyar, columnist)

Indrajit Gupta (Home)

Peaceful elections in Kashmir: "One has to give full credit to the home ministry for getting the National Conference to participate in the democratic process. Even making efforts to involve the Hurriyat Conference and other secessionist groups in the electoral process, should be commended," says Madhav Godbole.

Sarkaria Committee

Appointing of a standing committee to review the recommendations of the Sarkaria Commission which was set up to examine Centre-State relations was a welcome move. However, S.M. Murshed feels that it was only an academic exercise. "The decision to impose President's rule in any state is the President's. If there was to be a consultation in this matter between the Centre and the state, no state government would ever agree to be placed under President's rule."

Has the Home Minister been sidelined?

In two important instances — naming of Romesh Bhandari as UP governor and announcing of separate statehood for Uttarakhand — the Prime Minister did not consult the Gupta. Experts like Murshed feel, "If the PM persists, Gupta should resign."

Jumping the gun

Gupta has been criticised for speaking his mind even when his views are at cross purposes with the official policy, thus going against the norms of collective responsibility. The petroleum price hike and his remarks on the continuance of Narasimha Rao as Congress president, are cases in point. "His sincerity is refreshing but it is bound to confuse the public because he is holding a key position and is a member of a government which has a Common Minimum Programme which should guide policy," says Ribeiro.

Intelligence

The home ministry has not paid enough attention to the intelligence setup.

(Panelists: Madhav Godbole, former home sercetary; S.M. Murshed, adviser to the Governor, Jammu & Kashmir in 1993; Julio Ribeiro, former director general of police, Punjab)

Ram Vilas Paswan (Railways)

Man of the masses: His refusal to hike second-class passenger fares in the budget may be economically unsound but has been welcomed as a necessary welfare move. Introduction of more amenities on trains for the handicapped, the proposals to have telephone facilities and medical services available on long-distance trains and addition of new pantry cars to 11 trains has also been praised.

Unabashedly populist

The proposed setting up of six new railway zones, including one headquartered in Paswan's constituency, Hajipur, is completely populist. Most of the new railway lines and trains he has announced are also seen as either politically motivated or economically unviable.

Instead of concentrating on important issues like management of railway finances, safety, modernisation and increasing efficiency, the minister has promised to create new jobs in the railways as well as regularise 56,000 casual labourers. In an organisation that is already dangerously bloated, this is disastrous.

Privatisation on the backburner

Widely seen as a retrograde step. Apart from ordering a review of privatisation proposals, has already scrapped a contract awarded to a private party for the maintenance of New Delhi railway station.

Irresponsible

His removal of the ceiling on productivity linked bonus for railway employees led to the post and telegraph employees immediately demanding the same benefits and set off a chain reaction which played havoc with public services.

Hollow promises

The minister has, to date, been unable to initiate any solutions or even discussions on the terrible state of Mumbai's suburban railway system, despite the usual promises after taking over.

(Panelists: G.D. Patwardhan, railway historian; Dipak Gandhi, honorary secretary, Mumbai Suburban Railway Passengers Association, Raghu Dayal, ex-member, Railway Board)

S.R. Bommai (HRD)

Revival of literacy programmes: Among others, the total Literacy Campaign (TLC), which had degenerated after an initial zeal, has picked up.

Quick decision-making

Appointments to various organi-sations like the Indian Council for Social Science Research (ICSSR) and the University Grants Commission (UGC).

Adapting to market realities : The Technology Development Mission to promote industry-institute interaction by providing incentive for the industries, wherein industries now need to make only 25 per cent investment.

Cosmetic changes

Mere promotion of higher education by way of incentives in the form of grants to , say, the Indian Institutes of Technology

(IITs), is not enough. Failed to create an environment where the institutes can build up a corpus, while simultaneously cutting off funds to them.

Absence of long-term planning

An offshoot of uncertainty in funding. Vital sectors like education seem to develop in fits and starts, reflecting the way money is being made available to them.

Bleak campus scenarios

Has been unable to boost the morate at universities, which have become hotbeds of casteism and political rowdyism. Even today, a brilliant physicist/chemist/biologist will find himself jobless unless he/she is ready to switch to software or another, more 'applied' field. The number of research papers published by Indians has also decreased.

(*Panel: D.M. Nanjundappa, deputy chairman, Karnataka state planning board; G. Padmanabhan, director, Indian Institute of Science, K.R.S. Murthy, director, 11M, Bangalore)*

H.D. Deve Gowda (Prime Minister)

Political manager

Humphery Appleby described the British cabinet as "a loose confederation of warring tribes". The UF ministry, with more generals than soldiers, is similar. Deve Gowda, has been about as successful in "managing contradictions" — to use V.P. Singh's memorable phrase — as can be. His survival is his biggest achievement.

Speaking frankly

He once pleaded with gathered industrialists for help in furthering India's economy, saying, "Come to me with concrete proposals." Equally endearing was his lament that needless litigation delayed big projects. To quote Devaki Jain, "He has no time for fluff or windbags."

Let the law be

Courts and investigative agencies have taken on the gamut of politicians' — and even corporate houses - fairly unshackled.

Of course, most of what has been unearthed shows the previous government in poor light, so Gowda has no reason to complain — yet.

Cabinet at cross purposes

The pivot of the Union cabinet has succeeded politically, not administratively. "Gowda seems to be running an open government with a vengeance," says Madhav Godbole. Take Indrajit Gupta's big mouth, Mulayam singh Yadav's long absences from the defence ministry or Ram Vilas Paswan's profligate promises. The PM has been powerless to check these.

Bad PR

Notoriously unpunctual — he has even kept foreign dignitaries waiting — Gowda often goes to sleep at meetings or digs his nose. Took an enormous cluster of relatives to Harare and Rome.

Son of the soiled

Gowda's exaggerated interest in Karnataka politics needles CM J.H. Patel. Ordered the creation of a Karnataka regiment in the Army in violation of norms. Announced Bengalore's Hindustan Aeronautics would build passenger aircraft — riterating an old decision — and promptly called it his "gift to Karnataka".

Act now, think later

Surprised all by declaring the formation of Uttarakhand on the Independence Day. As Julio Ribeiro puts it, "He has acquired the unfortunate reputation of making hasty statements on delicate issues.

Went for a week to the north-east during the telecom strike. Though it was clear the workers' demands would be conceded, much of India couldn't communicate till the PM returned.

(From all the panelists, 17 have graded the PM)

C.M. Ibrahim (I&B; Civil Aviation)

Information & Broadcasting

Censoring news: After Ramakrishna Hegde was expelled from the Janata Dal, DD blacked out newsclips of people who spoke out against the move, from News Tonight and Aaj Tak.

Getting back at press

Announced a new defamation law after disclosures in the press about the dubious background of key figures in the Deve Gowda ministry, including Mohammad Taslimuddin and himself. Following widespread criticism, this was shot down.

Entertainment alone

Declared he would axe the loss-making DD-I and DD-India and restructure DD-III so that it would have no more commissioned programmes, only sponsored ones. Later on, Aaj Tak was moved to a later slot to make way for entertainment programmes, and its commercial tariffs increased five-fold. News Tonight was lost to STAR.

Contradictory action

Surprisingly for one obsessed with profits, dropped several money-spinners like Chandrakanta and replaced them with shoddy mythologicals with bad TRP ratings. All rules were bent to accommodate Ramanand Sagar's Sri Krishna the slot vacated by Chandrakanta.

Blinkered vision

Stymied an approval from the Foreign Investment Promotion Board to Pupert Murdoch's News Corp and declared he would impose legal restrictions on satellite channels to stop "He's a dangerous man to have at the helm of affairs, particularly in an area like information," says media commentator Sevaniti Ninan. "The move towards instituting the defamation law and his actions to stifle the News Corp initiative represent a draconian steak of expediency rather than conviction — we don't need that kind of cultural guardian."

Substandard DD

The bad coverage of events on the national channel continued. "The biggest failure was over the mid-air collision ot two planes," says Amita Malik. "DD was the last on the scene and outdoor by every other channel. This is a poor reflection on Mr. Ibrahim's revamping, if any, of his ministry, and symbolic of an attitude.

(Panclists: Amita Malik and Sevanti Ninan, media columnists)

Civil aviation

Too busy as PM's Man Friday

"The problems in this sector are challenging and need time and consideration," says an observer. Clearly the minister has neither, busy as he is being Deve Gowda's trouble shooter.

Blunder prone

Ibrahim's statement that domestic airlines would be barred from foreign equity is being seen as a move to protect Indian Airlines (IA) from competition. After deregulation in 1992, over 30 private operators came into operation. At the end of four years, only a handful survive. Ibrahim's statement has sent negative signals to foreign companies wishing to invest in this sector — the Tata-Singapore Airlines domestic airline project being a case in point.

He recently announced that the bodies of non-resident Indians who die in the Gulf will be transported free by Air India, Can AI, already in the red, absorb the cost of this goodwill gesture? And won't it set a precedent for other non-resident Indians? Subhash Goyal says such pronouncements are possible because of the lack of a proper civil aviation policy. "In its absence, the situation is open to ad hocism and the whims of the individual minister or secretary," he says.

Lack of moral responisbility

The fire that destroyed terminal IA at Delhi and the Saudia-Kazakh crash has taken place during Ibrahim's tenure. True, the causes were inherited, but shouldn't safety have been one of the first problems he addressed? "Safety, is a very deep-rooted problem that cannot be tackled cosmetically," says Air Marshall Denzil Keeler. Experts berate Ibrahim for not resigning after the tragedy. "It clearly reflects his lack of moral fibre," says an aviation expert.

(Panelists: Air Marshall Denzil Keeler, Rabindra Seth, tourism consultant, Subhash Goyal, travel consultant)

Murasoli Maran (Industry)

Small is big : A reform in the small-scale industrial sector is in the offing which could attract foreign participation and changes in the policy of reservation of items. "Most of the SSIs producing consumer goods will have to compete with the MNCs. If they are dereserved now, they would be open to domestic competition first. Otherwise having to suddenly compete with MNCs would wipe them out completely," says Mahesh Vyas.

The Foreign Investment Promotion Board has been taken out of the PMO and put under industry secretary, making FDI inflow speedier. "The ratio of inflow to approval in 1995-96 was 18 per cent, whereas it is 25 per cent now. The rate at which the government is clearing projects has also increased," says Vyas. Whatever time lag persists "is due to inhibiting factors like political uncertainty and states disapproving the FIPB's role, especially in the power sector," says Kiran Nanda, chief economist Gujarat Ambuja.

Potato Chips not a no-no : Contrary to the UF's common minimum programme objective of discouraging foreign investment in consumer goods and giving importance to infrastructural investment, Maran does not seem to differentiate between the two "There is nothing wrong with inviting investment to the consumer goods sector. It is better than the BJP's no to potato chip policy," says Kirit Parikh.

Drop in FDI

Because of the above hurdles, the government's stated preference for FDI overe FIIs has taken a beating. The going for the FIIs seems to be smoother than for FDI. In fact, the number of applications for setting up new projects has gone down.

Cart before the Horse

The proposed revival package for the 49 heavy industry PSUs of which 34 are loss-making and 25 are sick — is viewed by some as a sop to the Left.

(Panelists: Mahesh Vyas, director Centre for Monitoring the Indian Feconomy; Kirit Parikh, director, Indira Gandhi Institute for Deveelopment Resrearch: Kiran Nanda, Economist)

I.K. Gujral (External Affairs)

Principled stand on CTBT : This "earned India considerable respect in the comity of nations," says Bhabani Sen Gupta. While experts agree that a national consensus on the issue made it imperative for any government to sppose CTBT, instead of simply walking out of the conference — as the Rao regime might have done — Gujral took India's opposition to its logical end and blocked the treaty.

Good neighbourly relations : The ministry's constructive attitude towards its neighbours "is conducive to nurturing an atmosphere of stability and lessening of tensions in South Asia," says J.N. Dixit. For one, the two-year interim agreement with Bangladesh on the sharing of Ganga waters which is scheduled to be signed this month, will end a long and fractious dispute.

Despite India's delayed reaction to former Afghanistan president Najibullah's hanging by the Taliban forces, experts do not flay Gujral. In fact, they have praised him for not being involved in Afghanistan's internal affairs and for being included as a mediator to find a peaceful end to its civil war.

Natwar Singh calls Gujral's dignified approach towards Pakistan a "sensible attitude of benign neglect". Besides, with a democratically elected government in Kashmir and the promise of autonomy, "Kashmir is no longer an international issue," says Sen Gupta.

Security Council seat defeat

The fall-out of India's isolated stand on CTBT was the crushing defeat it received in the race against Japan for the non-permanent seat in the Security Council.

PM as ambassador

In the ultimate analysis, the prime minister of a country doubles up as a external affairs minister. In that context, Singh says, "Foreign affairs is a complex subject. Deve Gowda's whole conditioning is domestic."

(Panelists: Natwar Singh, foreign affairs expert; J.N. Dixit, retired IFS officer; Bhabani Sen Gupta, director, Centre of Studies in Global Change)

Annexure II

The Wrath of The Judges

Sunday; 10–16 November, 1996

Are nervous and angry politicians coming together to scuttle the courts' great cleansing drive?

At 8 p.m., on 26 September, after three reminders from his private assistant, Prime Minister Deve Gowda wound up a meeting with cabinet secretary T.S.R. Subramaniam and his own principal secretary Satish Chandran and left for the Krishna Menon Marg residence of the Chief Justice of India, A.M. Ahmadi, a short distance away. Three times they had fixed to meet and didn't, and Gowda was finally keeping his commitment the fourth time round.

Within a week, all manner of interpretation was given to that meeting. And 45 days on, the controversy has not quite died down. What did Deve Gowda discuss with the Chief Justice? "Routine" matters, as the Prime Minister's Office (PMO) and his law minister Ramakant Khalap, made it out to be? Or — as C.R. Irani, the editor of *The Statesman*, in a long signed piece, contends —did Gowda work up a scenario of superseding Justice J.S. Verma, most identified in the Supreme Court today with trying to rid corruption in politics and government?

Irani wrote on 4 October that the game plan seemed to be to have Ahmadi accept the chairmanship of the National Human Rights Commission, when the incumbent, former Chief Justice Ranganath Misra, retired on 15 October, and passing over number two judge Kuldip Singh and number three judge Verma, give his job to Justice M.M. Punchhi.

This cannot happen in normal course. Ahmadi retires on 25 March, 1997, and since Kuldip Singh retires before him, on 1

January, and Verma's term carries on till 18 January, 1998, Verma would have to be Chief Justice after Ahmadi. Irani revealed that if Ahmadi could be made to demit office before time, and a clause were introduced that a Chief Justice ought to have a minimum term of two years, then Verma would be bypassed and Justice Punchhi, number four in seniority now, made Chief Justice.

Irani said authoritatively that that was the whole point of the Prime Minister's meeting with the Chief Justice, and that the government had "full faith" in the judiciary and would see to it that it was not undermined but did not rebut the substance of Irani's charges.

Soon after, the Prime Minister, too, made a statement. "There is nothing unusual about my meeting with the Chief Justice and no unnecessary meaning should be read into it," he said ."...it was a routine meeting. Such meetings have taken place in the past also...during the meeting, there was absolutely no mention whatsoever of any matter pending in any court in the country or likely to come up on the judicial side."

"I know my responsibility and am quite conscious of the propriety involved and would never venture to broach any issue which is *sub judice* or is likely to arise in any court," he went on. "I also know that the Chief Justice of India would not tolerate any such talk." Like Khalap, however, he would not say if there had been — or still existed — a move to supersede Justice Verma.

But was there?

Inquiries reveal that the idea of superseding J.S. Verma was floated by a former Chief Justice who is close to Congress party bosses. The central aim was to somehow get Narasimha Rao off such cases as the St Kitts forgeries, the Jharkhand Mukti Morcha pay-offs and the Lakhubhai Pathak bribery scandal.

But since Narasimha Rao is not a very saleable figure nowadays, the former judge played upon fears of politicians who were scared of a sort of "judicial takeover" and angry with the courts, especially after S.N. Dhingra, the additional sessions judge, disallowed Kalpnath Rai, being tried in a TADA case, from attending Parliament and made scathing statements against politicians.

Chandra Shekhar, for instance, was livid then, and spoke his mind in Parliament. Atal Behari Vajpayee was moved, saying in the House, "...the court should respect Parliament and all the three wings of democracy — legislature, executive and judiciary — should have regard for each other." Even Somnath Chatterjee was pressed to say that Justice Dhingra had gone "beyond his jurisdiction and has made blanket criticism of each and every MP and the institution of Parliament. Nobody can condemn Parliament as a whole and we have to give a dignified response."

In this atmosphere of fear and anger, the former Chief Justice broached the subject of superseding Justice Verma, who has become a symbol of judicial activism, with several top politicians. One former Prime Minister was supportive, another was not keen even though he is soft on Narasimha Rao. Two Governors and a Congress chief minister were enthusiastic. And in Deve Gowda's government and party, several of the top men made it known that they would go along. Indrajit Gupta and Chaturanan Mishra were not consulted because they would never had agreed.

Politicians against judicial activism

P.V. Narasimha Rao:
Leads the pack. After the CBI filed charge-sheets against leading politicians in the Jain Havala case last year, he was wont to say, "The law will take its own course," to make out that he had no control over the events. Now, as he faces trial in the St Kitts scandal, the Jharkhand Mukti Morcha pay-offs and the Lakhubhai Pathak case, some of his men are making desperate attempts to ease things up for him.

The 12-October symposium on judicial activism held at the Parliament House Annexe at the behest of the Lok Sabha Speaker, P.A. Sangma, has such a background. Before it began, MPs from several political parties were very critical of the judiciary. And at the symposium itself, Sangma took a tough line. Rao's men are also trying to do some judicial fixing, but time is running out.

H.D. Deve Gowda

His dissatisfaction with the judiciary goes back to last year, when the Supreme Court jailed J. Vasudevan, an upright, secretary-rank officer of Karnataka, in a contempt petition. Gowda cried in the Assembly after having failed to meet the judge who had passed the sentence or to secure a presidential pardon. "They sent an honest man to jail," he said to MPs last month, "and I realised that the judiciary had to be shown its place."

Gowda has also told friends that he won't have a former Prime Minister — meaning Narasimha Rao — going to jail. This is not just because Rao's survival means longevity for his government. "He thinks that if a head of government is imprisoned," said an MP, "it will taint the political class forever and establish the supremacy of the judiciary over it."

Finally, Deve Gowda thinks that the courts are trying to take over the functions of the executive and he is especially cut up over attempts of the Patna High Court to direct the "Gawala" investigations against Laloo Prasad Yadav. "He doesn't particularly care if Laloo is indicted," said a senior bureaucrat in the cabinet secretariat. "But he says that he will resist any attempts of the courts to break the system." In this, at least, he has the backing of the bureaucracy.

Chandra Shekhar

The former Prime Minister has been upset with the judiciary since S.N. Dhingra, the additional sessions judge, made vicious remarks against politicians while denying Kalpnath Rai permission to attend Parliament. In a rare show of anger, he said, "This House should adjourn till we get an explanation from the judge. The Speaker must also consult the Chief Justice of India before convening the House again."

"I have never walked out of the House in my 24 years as a member," he went on, "but if the government does not take the stand on this, I will be forced to walk out." He didn't need to because, soon after, the Delhi High Court expunged portions of Justice Dhingra's judgement and admonished him. But Chandra Shekhar's anger has not abated.

When Rajesh Pilot spoke strongly in favour of the judiciary in Parliament, Shekhar apparently called him up in displeasure. "If Chandra Shekhar had been Prime Minister," said a lawyer close to Deve Gowda, cheekily, "he would have superseded Justice Verma just so as to shake up the judiciary."

V.C. Shukla

Has been identified as one of Rao's key aides who is running the battle against the judiciary. Has been charge-sheeted by the CBI for allegedly taking Havala money and would not be unhappy if the judiciary is "tamed". Has been remonstrating with Congress MPs who spoke in favour of judicial activism at the symposium.

Bhajan Lal

He has emerged as a major player in trying to get Narasimha Rao off the hook. He has "friend" in the higher judiciary and Congressmen say that he has not been in any way less active than the judiciary.

P.A. Sangma:

There is nothing direct to connect the Lok Sabha Speaker to moves to save Narasimha Rao. But his idea of holding a symposium has upset some judges and senior counsels. "The short agenda seems to be to protect the corrupt," said a top lawyer.

At the symposium, Sangma did not mince words criticising the judiciary. "Judges are but men of flesh and blood," he began. "They have indeed, on occasions, tended to be impacted by the media blitz on certain issues...there has been a tendency to take recourse to totally avoidable *obiter dicta*. This trend certainly smacks of judicial populism."

Some senior politicians suggested to Sangma that he might have gone a bit too far saying all this, and Sangma apparently conceded to them that he was "under pressure". The Speaker, himself, was unavailable for comment. He has greater support, however, for holding the view that the boundaries between the judiciary and the legislature/executive have to be more clearly laid out.

Laloo Prasad Yadav

His running with the judiciary began after the two Patna High Court judges, S.N. Jha and S.J. Mukhopadhyay, trying the "Gawala" case, directed the CBI director, Joginder Singh, to stay away from the investigation. He was asked not to "meddle in any manner in the investigation of the animal husbandry cases."

Singh had rejected a report prepared by the CBI's joint director (east), U.N. Biswas, naming Laloo Yadav as a "conspirator" and "abetter". A watered-down report was placed before the court instead which was rejected. The centre then filed petition against the High Court order in the Supreme Court that was heard on 31 October by a three-judge Bench headed by Justice Verma. It held that Biswas's report had been scuttled and warned Singh that it would not allow the probe to end up as a "sham exercise".

Mulayam Singh Yadav

There is no reason for him to be opposed to judicial activism except that his "friend", Satish Sharma, has been named in the Jharkhand Mukti Morcha case and also been show caused by the Supreme Court for allotting petrol pumps as petroleum minister.

It is not clear what Deve Gowda's position was. There is no paper trail as such. It is known that he has been unhappy with the judiciary since Justice K. Ramaswamy sent a Karnataka IAS officer, J. Vasudevan, to jail last year. Gowda was the chief minister of Karnataka then. George Fernandes told Sunday that he knows Deve Gowda wept before a Supreme Court judge.

He even wrote to the then home minister, S.B. Chavan, for a presidential pardon for Vasudevan and Narasimha Rao, then Prime Minister, asked his law minister, H.R. Bharadwaj, to help out. Bharadwaj says now that he told Rao that he could do little because it was a contempt case and that if a pardon was given now, judges would stop writing orders in future in protest. Gowda apparently went up to the President, and wept again before him. "But the President remained unmoved," revealed a senior bureaucrat in the PMO. Gowda returned embittered.

MPs who have spoken to Gowda at length say that he carried that grouse against the judiciary when he became Prime Minister. "He would get very emotional on the subject," said an MP. So when an idea was floated to supersede Justice Verma and thereby slow down the activism of courts, it couldn't have been unwelcome. But supersession itself, he knew, was not going to be simple.

N.K.P. Salve said last week that a constitutional amendment would be required to make a two-year term for a Chief Justice compulsory. "This will require two-thirds support in Parliament," he said. "Does Deve Gowda have that kind of support? Won't the Left and the Bharatiya Janata Party oppose it?"

If it comes to that, yes. "We will not allow it," L.K. Advani told *Sunday*. Even Rajesh Pilot made brave to say last week that he would resist it. But unhappiness against judicial activism cuts across party lines. "Barring the top two, nearly everyone in the BJP is against the activism of courts," said a top BJP lawyer. "If they just go ahead and decide to supersede without qualifications, then I cannot say, "conceded Salve.

But after the Supreme Court's nine-judges judgement of 1993, even that cannot happen without the concurrence of the Chief Justice. And there is nothing at all to suggest that Justice Ahmadi will approve any supersession. If anything, the meeting with Deve Gowda has caused him enormous embarrassment. The Supreme Court Bar Association took a vote on a resolution that"..in all fairness the Chief Justice of India should have avoided this meeting, keeping in view the highest tradition of this august institution." If it had been passed — as some say it was, and others say it was not — then he would have had to resign.

So, with all these stumbling blocks, how real was the move to oust Justice Verma? And, was it really a move or in the nature of a threat? It seems more likely the latter. And the threat remains.

The government has foreclosed the NHRC option for Justice Ahmadi, of course, former Chief justice M.N. Venkatachaliah is to be its next chairman. But the manner or announcement of his name is suspicious. It was made the same day that the SCBA vote against Ahmadi was due. The next day, Justice Venkatachaliah said to reporters that he had not been officially asked to take over. Last week, he told *Sunday* that he still hadn't been asked officially. Why not?

Then, there is still no denial that supersession plans were afoot. Irani said in his column that a statement that Justice Verma would be the next Chief Justice would quell all fears. It has not come. Last week, a senior official in the PMO said tantalisingly, "We will see in March when Justice Ahmadi's term expires." So the threat remains.

Lawyers from lower courts reckon that the threat might have already had effect on the higher judiciary. This is an unfair assessment but the charges persist. "The Supreme Court judgement exempting Narasimha Rao from personal appearance was unexpected," said Ashok Arora, counsel for Chandra Swami. Exception has also been taken to the judgement transferring the Lakhubhai Pathak case from Prem Kumar to Ajit Bharihoke. "It was a bad order," says Prashant Bhushan.

The order changing the venue of all trials concerning Narasimha Rao to Vigyan Bhavan on security grounds has also been criticised. "I took Indira Gandhi to Tis Hazari myself," says a former Congress minister. "And only this year, Narasimha Rao filed his nomination papers in a lower court in Delhi."

Even the Supreme Court order reinterpreting Section 438 of the Criminal Procedure Code in the St. Kitts case has drawn flak. A crucial paragraph says, "...anticipatory bail will ensue till the regular court decides the question of grant of bail and for a week thereafter so that if the regular courts, refuse bail, the accused persons can, if so advised, move the higher court." Chief Justice Ahmadi and Justice Verma passed this order at a sudden sitting in Justice Ahmadi's residence and lawyers say that the order is bizarre.

Last week, however, hearing the Centre's petition against the Patna High Court order removing the CBI director, Joginder Singh, from the "Gawala" investigation against Laloo Prasad Yadav, Justice Verma was his usually tough — and sober — self. While retaining Singh in the probe, he noted that an earlier CBI report critical of Laloo Yadav had been "scuttled". He made it clear that this would not be tolerated.

And just before Deve Gowda left for Harare, last week, he met the president of the SCBA, R.K. Jain, and his lawyer friend of ten years standing, Zille Singh Chauhan, at his office. "We told him that supersession was unacceptable to the bar and he listened to us," said Chauhan of their meeting. "He said that there will be no such move now." It was the final confirmation.

And yet, there is time still till March to take Deve Gowda for his word. Except that there is a bigger question mark about his own political survival till then.

Lending Respectability

Justice Venkatachaliah's guidelines helped insulate the judiciary against political interference

When M.N. Venkatachaliah retired as the Chief Justice of India two years ago, walked out of the Supreme Court, packed his bags and moved into his modest little house in Bangalore, many assumed that a distinguished career had come to an end. As it turned out, it didn't.

True, Justice Venkatachaliah, who is considered by many as one of the finest Chief Justices the country has ever seen, no longer hands down judgements. But one of the guidelines he set decides who gets to sit in the judges' and, for that matter, even the Chief Justice's chair.

In a couple of months, that legacy is expected to be put to the test when the current Chief Justice, A.M. Ahmadi, retires. The question is: who will be chosen as Ahmadi's successor? That the question is being raised at all reflects not only on today's scam-ridden politics but also on the increasing activism on the part of the judiciary.

One of Justice Venkatachaliah's path-breaking rulings concerned the process of selecting judges. Till 1980, when the S.P. Gupta case came up, the executive had primacy in the matter, and the scope for political interference this system allowed was not difficult to perceive.

However, Justice Venkatachaliah changed the rules. He not only held that the process should be reviewed but that the choice should be an institutional rather than a political or individual decision.

Under the guidelines he set, seniority gets importance in the appointment of the Chief Justice, and the selection of judges for all the courts in the country is based on the informed, verified and backed-up decisions of the Chief Justice of India. This leaves little space for governmental involvement.

Now, if Justice Venkatachaliah's rules are adhered to, Justice J.S. Verma should be the next Chief Justice of India. But given the fact that Justice Verma has rocked the political system by instituting an inquiry into the Havala scam, there is speculation now about the possibility of his being appointed to that post.

But Justice Venkatachaliah is not particularly worried. "The decision put the responsibility for the selection of judges, good or bad, on the judiciary," says Venkatachaliah. "Happily, not only have the choices been good so far, but there has been no violation of the guidelines in the recent past."

He has reasons to be optimistic. After all, he is the one who is credited for the respectability the judiciary presently enjoys. That is not only because of his high personal integrity but also for the decisions he took.

For instance, when the Havala scam first came before the Supreme Court in 1993, Justice Venkatachaliah ordered that a writ petition "should confine itself to judicial review of prosecutorial inaction." Today, when Justice Verma raps the CBI, it is because of the direction Justice Venkatachaliah gave the inquiry.

Justice Venkatachaliah, however, is surprisingly reticent about the path of activism that the judiciary is taking. Though he seldom speaks to the press about it, he expressed reservations in a speech made last year at the International Bar Association in Bombay. Cautioning the judiciary against taking on the role of the executive, he said that the four pillars of democracy should grow together.

"Can judicial wisdom really be the panacea for everything?" he wonders when asked about judicial activism, and adds, "Instead of being suspicious or uncharitable about everything, I would prefer some amount of honest gullibility. If anything happens in the judiciary, I would like to assume that they were because of bonafide reasons."

Annexure III

Speech by Dr. Shankar Dayal Sharma President of India

(At the Inauguration of the Golden Jubilee Celebrations of the Constitution of the Constituent Assembly held at Vigyan Bhawan, New Delhi, Monday, December 9, 1996, 18 Agrahayana, 1918 (Saka))

It gives me immense pleasure to associate myself with the Golden Jubilee celebrations of the first sitting of the Constituent Assembly organized by the Supreme Court Bar Association. I thank the Hon'ble Chief Justice of India, Shri A.M. Ahmadi and the President of the Bar Association, Shri R.K. Jain for their thoughtful invitation to me.

It is most appropriate that the Bar Association should have organized this function to commemorate this important anniversary. So many of our great national leaders who contributed to the fashioning of our Constitution were jurists of distinction. The many finely trained legal minds who participated in the deliberations of the Constituent Assembly included: Dr. Rajendra Prasad, Pandit Jawaharlal Nehru, Dr. Babasaheb Ambedkar, Sardar Patel, Shri Govind Vallabh Pant, Shri K.M. Munshi, Shri Alladi Krishnaswami Ayyar, Shri B.N. Rau, Shri B.L. Mitter, Shri S. Varadachariar, Shri Kailash Nath Katju, Smt. G. Durgabai and Shri M.A. Ayyangar.

The Bar Association is heir to a rich tradition of service to the nation in the spheres of social and political advancement through the building and operation of a sensitive and responsive judicial system. I am glad, therefore, that they are undertaking a series of programmes and seminars throughout the year in order to create more widespread public awareness about the historic and magnificent work of the Constituent Assembly, the significance of our Constitution, and the very tangible manner in which it is contributing to the progress and prosperity of our society.

Our long and arduous struggle for freedom was essentially a struggle for the Rule of Law, a struggle for the values of equality, respect for human dignity and justice. It drew sustenance from our ancient ethos of toleration and respect for diverse points of view, of pluralism and oneness, of consensus and mutual accommodation. 'Dharma' or the Rule of Law, has been recognized as vital for the well-being of our society. As stated in the Karna Parva of the Mahabharata, Verse 58, Chapter 69:

धारणाद् धर्मामित्याहुर्धर्मो धारयते प्रजा: ।

यत् स्याद् धारणसंयुक्तं स धर्म इति निश्चय: ।

(Dharma is for the stability of society, the maintenance of social order and the general well-being and progress of humankind. Whatever conduces to the fulfilment of these objects is Dharma : that is definite.)

Indeed it is most appropriate that the motto of the Supreme Court of India is:

"यतो धर्मस्ततो जय"

(Where there is fulfilment of Dharma, there is (Supreme) Victory).

The Judiciary has the vital function of upholding Dharma.

Our Constitution recognized the pivotal importance of the Judiciary, as the guardians of the Constitution. This profound awareness was expressed in beautiful and telling words by Pandit Jawaharlal Nehru while speaking in the Lok Sabha on 14th March, 1955, he said:

> "...the fundamental basis of this Constitution and our general practice in this country is to have an independent and powerful judiciary."

Panditji stressed the need for the independence of the judiciary and its being powerful. There was unanimity in the Constituent Assembly that it was essential to have a completely independent Judiciary, 'an impregnable fortress,' as it were, impervious to present and beyond reproach. The experience of our leaders during colonial rule strengthened the demand for a separation of the Executive from the Judiciary. Article 50 of the Directive Principles of State Policy articulated this concern.

"The State shall take steps to separate the judiciary from the executive in the public services of the State."

The founding fathers paid meticulous attention to the task of ensuring and safeguarding the independence of the judiciary, its jurisdiction and powers, the calibre and status of those manning it and their conditions of tenure. The various provisions of the Constitution in Chapter IV of Part V of the Constitution and Chapter V of Part VI of the Constitution reflect the determination and clarity of vision with which the founding fathers accomplished their task in this respect.

Another perception of profound significance to our polity arising out of the deep awareness and farsighted perspective of the Constituent Assembly, was the idea of a unified Judiciary, as an institutional framework which would contribute solidly to the strengthening of national unity and oneness. It is such remarkable insight into the inner processes of our Parliamentary Democracy, the mechanics of the day-to-day working of our polity, that informs a brilliant observation by the Chairman of the Drafting Committee, Dr. Babasaheb Ambedkar. He said:

> "one single integrated judiciary having jurisdiction and providing remedies in all cases under the Constitutional law, the Civil Law or the Criminal Law . . . ." is ". . . .essential to maintain the unity of our country."

The Constitution of India has provided the framework within which individual rights are safeguarded and social well-being is enhanced. It has established a harmonious balance between the rights of the individual and the good of society as a whole. The Right to Constitutional Remedies enshrined in Article 32 of our Constitution provides for the enforcement of the provisions of Part III on Fundamental Rights. The writ jurisdiction of the Supreme Court and its powers to issue directions or orders or writs confers a role of profound importance on the court. Indeed, I have often said that the Supreme Court of India is a bulwark for safeguarding human rights. I would, in particular, mention Article 13 which declares void laws inconsistent with or in derogation of the Fundamental Rights. Simultaneously, the concept of 'reasonable restrictions' has been refined and developed to make for a judicious synthesis of individual and public or national interest.

Over the last five decades or so, the Judiciary has played a role of far reaching significance in deealing with the relationship between Law and the lives of individuals and of society. The Judiciary administers the Law but equally, and in some cases, more importantly, the judiciary also makes Law in the context of our common law system, including our system of precedents. Judicial interpretation of provisions of our Constitution and the laws has resulted in a series of decisions that have safeguarded and upheld the national, public and individual interest, fundamental human freedoms and the cause of Justice. By consistently, sensitively, and expertly, interpreting the provisions of the Constitution and the laws, in tune with the requirements of justice, the Supreme Court has helped magnify the majesty of law in giving relief to members of the public, and thus, in the aggregate, making for a better and safer quality of life for our nation.

As I indicated earlier, our Constitution encapsulates the vision of our society for progress, prosperity and emancipation. It is the vision of 'Purna Swaraj' in all its varied dimensions. The Constitution and the laws are essential catalytic entities in this dynamic striving of the people for a better life.

Dr. Babasaheb Ambedkar and other members of the Constituent Assembly had held the firm conviction that Law is an instrument for social change; that Law synthesizes change and stability; that Law must be a 'variable constant'; that Law subsists on the basis of objective appreciation of truth and social good.

Pandit Jawaharlal Nehru while speaking on the Draft Constitution on 8th November, 1948 had expressed these ideas thus:

> "The Constitution if it is out of touch with the people's life, aims and aspirations becomes rather empty; . . . a Constitution should...be flexible."

Later in May, 1951 he had said:

> "A Constitution to be living must be growing; must be adaptable; must be flexible; must be changeable . . . Therefore, it is desirable and a good thing for people to realize that this very fine Constitution that we have fashioned after years of labour is good in so far as it goes but as society changes, as

conditions change we amend it in the proper way. It is not like the unalterable law of Medes and Persian that it cannot be changed, although the world around may change".

The Judiciary, and in this term I would include members of the Bar, have vindicated Panditji's philosophy. They have ensured that Law advances the cause of social welfare in a tangible and effective manner in our society. Without amendments to the Constitution also, through interpretation of the law, the judiciary has been instrumental in the process of Law adapting itself commensurate to the needs of changing times. Many landmark decisions on matters of public interest, like those relating to environmental issues, greater transparency and accountability of administration, have made an enduring impact on our society.

The Bar should be recognized as an integral component of the judiciary. The Bench and the Bar, together, comprise the judicial mechanism. It is their joint duty, their 'Dharma', to exemplify and give effect to the inextricable and organic link between Law, Truth and Social Welfare. It is their responsibility to ensure that these noble goals are always upheld.

Acumen, knowledge, commitment and high moral and ethical stature of the Bar are critical to the appropriate functioning of our judicial system. By forceful articulation of cases and the ability to separate the grain from the chaff, the Bar should assist in the cause of Justice by bringing forth Truth and nothing but the Truth before the Court. I am glad that we have developed and drawn upon the concept of 'Amicus Curiae', friend of the Court - whereby members of the Bar are to assist the Court in comprehending and assessing the facts of any case, the relevant law and its particular application in the matter and identifying the appropriate view or remedy as required.

India is proud of her active, strong and independent Judiciary. Our learned judges and members of the Bar have lived up to the expectations of the people and have strengthened our democratic policy.

I am sure that in the years and decades ahead the Bench and the Bar in India will go from strength to strength in achieving greater and greater success in the service of the nation, the cause of Justice, the goal of building a Welfare State, and a society corresponding to the dreams of those who gave their all in the struggle for freedom and who laboured in the Constituent Assembly of India five decades ago.

With these words, I have great pleasure in inaugurating your celebrations. I wish you all every success in your endeavours in the months and years ahead.

Jai Hind

Annexure IV

Strengthen Polity, says President

Pioneer News Service, New Delhi

President Shankar Dayal Sharma on Monday called upon the people to think of ways to improve the working of the institutions of India's democratic polity.

He told the Members of Parliament and other dignitories, at a function in the Central Hall of Parliament to commemorate the 50th anniversary of the first sitting of the Constituent Assembly, that the meaning and import of the Constitution should be brought closer to the common man.

"This would be possible if we take up the challenge of making our institutions, our administration and systems of work, directly accountable and fully mindful and sensitive to the needs and feelings of our people," he said.

Among those present on the occasion were eight of the 15 surviving members of the Constituent Assembly, to whom the President gave away momentoes. They were Mr. S. Nijalingappa, Mr. C. Subramaniam, Begum Aizaz Rasool, Chaudhary Ranbir Singh, Mr. Motiram Baigra, Mr. Kusum Kant Jain, Mr. Balwant Singh Mehta and Mr. Bhagwan Din.

Dr. Sharma said : "If we look at nations around us, we can be proud of our resilient, living Constitution which has adpated over time, to changing circumstances, needs and requirements. Indeed, it has become a model for constitutions in other countries."

As the country prepared to step into a new century and millenia let us ask ourselves what our goals and tasks are as citizens . . . . what are our responsibilities in nation building...and how best we can discharge them . . . . let us draw inspiration from Bapu's life and work and live up to his message of 'Anashakti' and 'Nishkaam Karm' or selfless service i.e. service without regard to the fruits of action," said Dr. Sharma.

"This anniversary provides an opportunity for every citizen of India to renew the pledge to work for 'Purna Swaraj', for the well being of our people, for peace and harmony in our society and indeed the world," concluded the President.

Prime Minister H.D. Deve Gowda said with independence, the political revolution ended, but the social and economic revolution had still to run their course.

"Political freedom will be meaningless without economic and social rights," he said, adding political freedom was not an end but the means to achieve social and economic equality.

He said almost 50 years after freedom. India today still stood at the crossroads, with its development lopsided, haunted by spectres of unemployment and poverty and the goals of social and economic equality still very distant.

"We have achieved political equality, but social justice still seems to elude people" he said. The State has to promote welfare and bring about social order where justice was a part of normal life, he said.

Paying tributes to the Constituent Assembly, he said it gave a "wonderful political and legal device" for the common man by enshrining the aspirations of the people of India.

"We must ask ourselves have we failed the Constitution," the Prime Minister said, adding "we have to ponder over what we have done and not done for the country" and whether "we had redeemed the promise of our forefathers of a vibrant India."

Mr. Gowda said though the Constitution was amended at least 78 times, the country had not been able to achieve the cherished goals of economic and social emancipation.

He reiterated the United Front Government's commitment to give one-third reservation to women in Parliament and State legislatures.

In his address, Vice President K.R. Narayanan said the political scene today was in a state of fragmentation "like a broken mirror" but the image in each fragment was that of a unified India "is it possible to put back the pieces," he asked.

He said the current deterioration in values and standards could only be stemmed by a determined Parliament.

Today, when there was a need for a unifying force, Parliament was one body which could create a consensus on all issues, he said.

"Today, Indian politics is facing a crisis of values and a crisis of standards of behaviour."

"If we turn our attention to this basic question and reflect upon possible ways in which this deterioration can be stemmed, we would have celebrated the Golden Jubilee of the first meeting of the Constituemt Assembly in a meaningful manner," said the Vice President.

Lok Sabha Speaker P.A. Sangma said one of the public debates today concerned the future of the Parliamentary form of Government.

The framers of the Constitution after giving serious thought to presidential form of Government, opted for a Parliamentary form on the conviction that "in our conditions, responsibility of the executive should be given paramount consideration."

Annexure V

In the High Court of Delhi

C.M. 5068/96 IN CW 2408/96
Date of Decision: November 21, 1996.

Janak Raj Jai .... In - Person
Versus
Shri H.D. Deve Gowda & Others .... Mr. Ashok Desai, Attorney General with Mr. A.K. Wali for the UOI & Mr. Keshav Dyal, Advocate

Coram :
Hon'ble Mr. Justice Jaspal Singh
Hon'ble Mr. Justice J.K. Mehra

Jaspal Singh, J.

On July 5, 1996 we had dismissed the writ petition filed by Dr. Janak Raj Jai challenging the appointment of Shri H. Deve Gowda as the Prime Minister of India. The ground urged was that Shri Deve Gowda being not a member of either House of Parliament, the President could not have made the said appointment.

On July 30, 1996 was moved this petition for review of our order on the ground that Shri Deve Gowda, being a sitting Member of the Legislative Assembly, Karnatka, could not be sworn the oath of office of the Prime Minister of India and that consequently his appointment to the said office was "bad in law, void abinitio and in violation of the Provisions of the Constitution of India."

Though Shri Deve Gowda bestrides the story, the learned Attorney General who appeared for him adopted the strategy of distancing him from us, as F. Scott Fitzgerald did in the Great Gatsby, by forwarding the argument that the review petition itself was not maintainable and by making a plea that we should proceed to decide the said objection first. Since Dr. Jai had no objection, the arguments centred around the said objection only.

One thing is certain, and on that we entertain no doubt, that there is nothing in Article 226 of the Constitution of India to preclude the High Court from exercising the power of review which, as repeatedly held by the Supreme Court, inheres in every Court of plenary jurisdiction to prevent misscarriage of justice or to correct grave and palpable errors committed by it. But then the power is neither boundless nor unfeterred. It has its own boundaries, well carved and definitive. One of the situations envisaging exercise of this power is where a new and important matter or evidence is discovered but then, this would be subject to the condition that it was not within the knowledge of the person seeking review even after the exercise of due diligence. We do not propose to travel on to the other situations calling for exercise of the power as Dr. Jai had sought refuge under none other than the one enumerated above.

It was argued that the fact that Shri Gowda was a member of the Legislative Assembly of Karnataka came to be known only after the dismissal of the writ petition. The source of information, we are told, was a press report published in the Hindu dated July 6, 1996.

Does this fall within the parameters of the situation delineated above?

Before we proceed to answer the question posed above, let us extract that portion of the review petition which deals with the assertion. This is how the petitioner puts it:

> "4. That there is a discovery of new fact, which was not available at the time of filing the present petition (sic) in this Hon'ble Court that from a press report published in Hindu dated 6.7.1997, the petitioner came to know that respondent No. 1, Shri Deve Gowda, had been a Member of Legislative Assembly, Karnataka, at the time when an oath of Prime Minister was being administered to him by the President. He had resigned from Chief Ministership, but he continues to be a Member of the Legislative Assembly, till this day, as

> is reported in the Hindu. This point could not be pleaded in the main writ petition due to lack of information."

Let us assume that the information relates to an important matter. Let us also accept, for arguments sake, the assertion of the petitioner that he came to know of it only on July 6, 1996, that is, after the disposal of the writ petition. Does it make out a case for review? The answer has to be simply in the negative.

Let us recollect what we said earlier. It was, and we repeat, that the power of review may be exercised where a new and important matter or evidence is discovered which was not within the knowledge of the person seeking review even after the exercise of due diligence. Where, pray, is even the bare assertion of exercise of due diligence? Where are we told, what to talk of being assured, that the petitioner had in fact exercised reasonable care and diligence? Surely, mere assertion that the information was received subsequent to the disposal of the writ petition cannot itself be taken to show that due diligence could not have been exercised: otherwise there cannot be any case coming within this rule. What is required is strong evidence of diligence and what to talk of such strong evidence, there is not even a bald assertion to that effect. The condition surely is very strict and it is enacted so as to prevent litigants lying on their oars when they ought to be looking for evidence. The petitioner meets his waterloo on this ground alone.

This, however, is still not the end of the matter.

Admittedly, the petitioner had alrady filed an appeal in the Supreme Court against our order of dismissal of the writ petition and admittedly again, that appeal is still pending. This being the position should we proceed to entertain this petition for review? This is what the Privy Council says in (Raja) Indrajit Pratap Bahadur Sahi v. Amar Singh and others AIR 1923 PC 128 :

> "Where an appeal has been preferred, a review is out of question and the party's proper course is to apply to the appellate Court may for any other substantial cause viz., other than those particularly specified allow such evidence or documents to be produced or witnesses to be examined. Rules of procedure are not made for the purpose of hindering justice."

We need say no more.

And lastly what is sought to be urged is a new ground. It was, we feel, rightly contended by the learned Attorney General that no new ground can be allowed to be urged through the corridors of a review petition. The proposition finds support from the judgment of the Supreme Court in Collector of 24 Parganas vs. Lalith Mohan Mullick AIR 1988 SC 2121.

A word more before the curtain is finally drawn. The petitioner had sought amendment of the main writ petition seeking to incorporate the new ground. Mecrifully, during arguments, the petitioner did not choose to press it and thus saved himself from yet another frustrating result and us from another legal Tae Kwon Do and resultant dreary fatigue.

For the reasons recorded above, we see no reason to entertain this review petition which accordingly fails and is dismissed.

SD./-
(Jaspal Singh)
Judge.

SD./-
(J.K.Mehra)
Judge

Annexure VI

In the Supreme Court of India

Civil Appellate Jurisdiction

Special Leave Petition (C) No. 19606 of 1996

Dr. janak Rai Jai		Petitioner
	Vs.	
Sh. H.D. Deve Gowda		Respondent

ORDER

The petitioner had filed a writ petition in the Delhi High Court being CWP No. 2408/96 challenging the appointment of Sh. H.D. Deve Gowda as the Prime Minister of India on the ground that his appointment was not legal and proper since he was not a Member of either House of Parliament. Since the writ petition was dismissed by the High Court. the petitioner has come before us by way of the present special leave petition.

A similar contention was urged before us in a writ petition filed under Article 32 of the Constitution of India by S.P. Anand. By our judgment and order in that matter. being S.P.Anand vs. H.D. Deve Gowda reported in (1996) 6 SCC 734, we have given detailed reasons for rejecting the petition. The basic question which is posed by the present petitioner is the same — Can a person who is not a Member of either House of Parliament be sworn in as the Prime Minister of India? After comparing in detail Articles 74 and 75 of the Constitution with Articles 163 and 164 of the Constitution, it has been observed in the above judgment as follows:

"Now Article 75(1) envisages a Council of Ministers with the Prime Minister at the head to aid and advise the President, and the latter is expected to act in accordance with such advice but if he has any reservations he may require the Council of Ministers to reconsider such advice. Thus, the President has to act in accordance with the advice of the Council of Ministers as a body and not go by the advice of any single individual. Only a person who, the President thinks. Commands the confidence of the Lok Sabha would be appointed the Prime Minister who in turn would choose the other Ministers. The Council of Ministers is made collectively responsible to House of the People. The form of the oath prescribed in the Third Schedule under Article 75(4) is the same for the Prime Minister as well as a Minister. In other words, the Constitution does not draw any distinction between the Prime Ministers and any other Minister in this behalf. This is not to say that the Prime Minister does not enjoy a special status; he does as the head of the Council of Ministers but the responsibility of the Council of Ministers to the House of the People is collective, besides, the caption of Article 75 as a whole is "Other provisions as to Ministers". No separate provision is to be found dealing with the appointment of the Prime Minister as such. Therefore, even though the Prime Minister is appointed by the President after he is chosen by such number of members of the House of the People as would ensure that he has the confidence of the House and would be able to command the support of the majority, and the Ministers are appointed on the advice of the Prime Minister, the entire Council of Ministers is made collectively responsible to the House and that ensures the smooth functioning of the democratic machinery. If any Minister does not agree with the majority decision of the Council of Ministers, his option is to resign or accept the majority decision. If he does not, the Prime Minister would drop him from his Cabinet and thus ensure collective responsibility. Therefore, even though a Prime Minister is not a member of either House of Parliament, once he is appointed he becomes answerable to the House and so also his Ministers and the principle of collective responsibility governs the democratic process. Even if a person is not a member of the House, if he has the support and confidence of the House, he can be chosen to head the Council of Ministers without violating the norms of democracy and the requirement of being accountable to the House would ensure the smooth functioning of the democratic process." Dealing with the British convention that the Prime

Minister should be a Member of either House. preferably `the House of Commons, it has been observed therein that this is not our Constitutional scheme since our Constitution clearly permits a non-Member to be appointed a Chief Minister or a Prime Minister for a short duration of six months. That is why in such cases when there is any doubt in the mind of the President, he normally asks the person appointed to seek a Vote of Confidence of the House of People within a few days of his appointment. The contentions which have been urged by the petitioner, therefore, do not survive in the light of this judgement.

The Petitioner, however, applied before the High Court of Delhi for a review of its impugned judgment on the ground that he had subsequently discovered that after being appointed as the Prime Minister of India. Sh. Deve Gowda had retained his Membership of the Karnataka Legislative Assembly. He resigned from his Membership of the Karnataka Legislative Assembly on becoming a Member of the Rajya Sabha. The High Court of Delhi rightly rejected the review petition since in a review petition, such new grounds could not be urged. The petitioner has challenged the rejection of this ground before us.

In order not to leave any grievance, we briefly deal with this additional submission also. Under Article 75(5), a person who is not a Member of either House of Parliament can be appointed a Minister for a period of six consecutive months. If during this period he is not elected to either House of Parliament he will cease to be a Minister. We have not been shown any Article of the Constitution under which a person who is elected to a State Legislature is prohibited from being appointed as a Minister under Article 75(5). In fact, Article 75(5) is widely worded. It covers every person who is not a Member of either House of Parliament such a person can be appointed as a Minister and can remain as a Minister only for a period of six consecutive months unless he is elected to either House of Parliament within that period. If he is not so elected, he shall cease to be a Minister on the expiry of six consecutive months. The same provision is applicable to the Prime Minister for reasons which we have set out in our judgment in the case of S.P. Anand (supra). There is no disqualification which can be spelled out under Article 75(5) in respect of a Member of a State Legislative Assembly, who is appointed under Article 75(5).

The contention that "his willingness and desire of becoming a Member of Parliament comes under cloud" if he is a Member of the Legislative Assembly has to be only stated to be rejected.

Briefly put, all the contentions urged in the present petition except the contention in regard to the rejection of the review application were considered in SP Anand's case (supra) after considering the Constitutional scheme in that behalf. As far as the rejection of the review application is concerned, we think that the High Court was right in doing so.

The petition is, therefore, dismissed. There will, however, be no order as to costs.

24.1.1997
Arvind Kumar
Laxmi Arvind
A.L. Trehan
K.K. Sharma
Rajiv Jai
Kiran Jai
(Advocates for the petitioner)

A.M. Ahmadi
C.J.
Sujata V. Manohar
G.B. Pattnaik
J.J

The Dramatic Fall and the Constitutional Breakdown

On 30th March, 1997 the Congress President, Sitaram Kesri, all of a sudden withdrew the support of his party from the United Front Government, charging them that the government headed by Deve Gowda had failed to contain the communal forces and had also ignored his party while taking policy decisions. Not only this, the Congress President dubbed Deve Gowda as *nikamma* (incompetent) and a communalist having met Bal Thakrey mysteriously. A letter of withdrawing the support of the Congress Party was delivered to the President of India the same day, i.e. on 30.3.1997.

It was certainly a bolt from the blue for the constituents of the United Fornt, as they never expected that the Congress Party would take such a drastic step so suddenly, particularly at a time when talks between India and Pakistan were going on, and the NAM Meeting was to be held in the beginning of April 1997. At the same time the Senior Congress Leaders were taken aback, as many of them were unaware of the withdrawal of support by the Congress. The Leader of the Congress Parliamentary Party in Lok Sabha, Sharad Pawar is on record to say that he had no knowledge of the withdrawal of the Congress support from the UF Government. In fact he was not in Delhi when the letter of withdrawal of support was sent to the President of India. The President then asked the Prime Minister to seek a vote of confidence on 7.4.1997, on the floor of the House. But on the request of the Prime Minister, the date was extended to 11th April 1997.

On 11th of April, 1997, there was a marathon debate on the confidence motion moved by the Government headed by Deve

Gowda. The debate started at 11 A.M. and continued until after 11 P.M., when ultimately the motion was rejected by 292 votes as against 158 in favour of the motion. So the end of this government came after 11 months on 11th April at about or after 11 P.M. The whole world watched the proceedings as there was complete arrangement of the live programme. The stalwarts including Atal Behari Vajpayee, Chandra Shekhar, Shiv Raj Patil, Somnath Chatterji, Banatwala, Nitish Kumar, Indrajit Gupta, Rajesh Pilot, Surjit Singh Barnala, Uma Bharti and many more put up their points of view. The performance of almost all the speakers was excellent and is a valuable piece of history. The Speaker, P.A. Sangma and his deputies managed the whole show in a very dignified manner and by and large the members of different political parties cooperated with the chair keeping in view the seriousness of the debate in the august House.

Last but not the least, Deve Gowda's performance was superb. He defended his case excellently and with full confidence. Here are some highlights:

Gowda's last words as PM

(1) I need no certificate from Kesri
(2) I have no problem. I will go to the other House. I have five years to stay.
(3) If destiny is there, I will rise from the dust, and come back here. I will not run away from Indian Politics.
(4) When you are charging me with making attempts to divide the Congress, what moral courage do you have to divide the United Front by suggesting that a new leader be chosen in my place.
(5) I will go to the people and come back to power. I am going to show what Deve Gowda is.
(6) There is no need for any manipulative politics. The people of this country are aware of manipulative politics.
(7) I have contested ten elections. Has Mr. Kesri fought any direct election in his life?
(8) Am I responsible for the Congress defeat in Punjab, in corporation election in Maharashtra and in several other by elections?

(9) In the last ten months, all the steps taken by the United Front Government have clearly proved that UF Government is better than the previous governments.

A resigned people watch the day's events:

"Whether it was the panwallah or rikshawallah or the businessman, Delhiites fought the heat and long speeches in Parliament to keep abreast of the news of nation's immediate future.

People were seen glued to radio sets and gathering around shops with TVs switched on. Even in buses, the topic of conversation remained, "Who is happy at the fall of the government, and why?

But there were those who did not seem to care a fig. A bus conductor thought he was more efficient than the politician as he has retained his job for more than two years now."

Courtesy: Times of India, 12.11.97

I was sitting in the Coffee Home and had been listening to the reaction of the public on the fall of the Government.

Roop Narayan, a veteran freedom fighter and a staunch follower of JayaPrakash Narayan said, "It was the CPI(M) mainly Harkrishan Singh Surjeet, who was the main spokesman of the UF Government and the Congress party which has the largest number of M.P.s has been completely marginalised. Why should the Congress party allow the UF Government to work and get every credit at their cost. The UF Government did not support Mayavati simply to please Mulayam Singh Yadav and turned down the request of Sita Ram Kesri and allowed Romesh Bhandhari to play their game."

On the other hand, a political activist, V.K. Dogra said, "It was under pressure from America that Advani and Kesri chalked out a plan to throw out Deve Gowda's Government. The American Ambassador had secret parleys with Kesri and Advani.

Here are some flashes on the political scenario, one day after the fall of Deve Gowda Government:

The day after

Overnight

- Political cliff-hanger, Gowda loses trust vote, resigns. Is caretaker PM. Tough task ahead for United Front. Find alternative, keep flock together, sidestep polls.

Morning

- Steering panel meets.
- Moopanar, Karunanidhi, Mulayam stick to guns. Want change; soft on Congress.
- Gowda refuses to throw in towel. Basu stands by PM, ready to seek mandate.
- Naidu, Bardhan, Surjeet neutral. Want solidarity.
- Moopanar tells chidambaram to find way out.
- Vajpayee to weigh BJP's possibilities.
- Fine, say Kanshi, Fernandes.

Before Noon

- Karunanidhi, Maran brief VP.
- VP pleads for unity.
- Kesri not in race to be PM. Wants new front leader.

Afternoon

- Surprise call for Kesri, Gowda on line, thanks for past support.
- Storm brewing at Pawar's house. MPs from both Houses get together for tea.
- Actually, Mamata challenge Kesri, demand CPP meet.
- Pawar asked to decide future.
- Pranab, Karunakaran, Azad leave in huff.
- Pawar, Azad, Chavan brief Kesri

Evening

- Front constituents sign letter to President. No support to Congress, BJP.

Night

- Bid to stem revolt. CWC meet on Monday; Tariq announces CPP meet on April 20.

- Steering panel meet again.
- Moopanar, Karunanidhi stay away.
- No change, says Reddy.
- Issue unsolved, steering panel to meet today

Chronology of the Gowda Government

June 1, 1996: UF Government assumes office under the premiership of Deve Gowda, The Congress Party, with 145 members of Parliament, extends unconditional support from outside.

October 16, 1996: UF declines support to the Congress for forming the Government with BSP in U.P.

February 12, 1997: Congress changes its original stand and converts the unconditional support into an issue based backing,

March 30, 1997: Congress President withdraws the support and hands over the letter of withdrawal to the President of India.

March 31, 1997: President tells Deve Gowda to seek a vote of confidence on the floor of the House on 7th April, 1997. But the date was later on extended to 11th April.

April 2, 1997: Lok Sabha announces one day session for the UF to seek a vote of confidence.

April 3, 1997: UF and Congress hold informal talks.

April 4, 1997: Deve Gowda meets Jyoti Basu and V.P. Singh in Apollo Hospital.

April 5, 1997: Kesri calls Gowda nikamma (inefficient) and communal.

April 6, 1997: BJP declares its stand opposing the motion of confidence.

April 7, 1997: Akali Dal toes the BJP line and declares to oppose the motion.

April 8, 1997: UF proposes formal talks with Congress to resolve the crisis.

April 9, 1997: UF and Congress hold formal talks. UF rejects the Congress demand for a change of leadership.

April 10, 1997: Second round of talks failed. Congress issues whip to the members to vote against the motion.

April 11, 1997: Marathon Debate continued till 11.30 P.M. The motion was defeated with 158 in favour, and 292 against. U.F. Government thus comes to an end after 11 months of the installation.

Constitutional Breakdown

The dramatic fall of Deve Gowda Government has created a constitutional break down and there is a great challenge for the President to overcome the crisis. Whether the President is bound to accept the advice of the outgoing Prime Minister, under these circumstances, is not very clear in the Constitution. The Constitutional Exports are also baffled and have come out with their own view points on the discretionary powers and the subjective satisfaction of the President while dealing with such a situation. Almost all of them agree that the Constitution does not specifically mention anything on the issue.

Former Secretary General of the Lok Sabha, C.K. Jain, is of the view that the President can look for alternatives, after the fall of the Government. Supreme Court lawyer P.P.Rao also agreed that 'the President would be justified in exploring the possibility of alternative governments. However he added that the President should only allow a party to stake its claim, after being satisfied that it has reasonable hopes of mustering majority support. Describing the BJP's short-lived government as an "unfortunate and unhealthy precedent", he remarked that the President should have found out whether the BJP had the requisite majority to form the government. "Keeping in mind the possibility that the next elections may return the same verdict as in 1996, it would be an act of statesmanship if the President looks out for a National Government."

According to a Çonstitutional Laywer K.K. Venugopal 'President's diserctionary power in regard to dissolution of the House is an integral and indispensable rule of the Parliamentary system envisaged in the Constitution. It is , therefore, logical to construe "shall" in Art. 74(1) not in the absolute sense otherwise it might result in further complication in the functioning of the parliamentary system.'

According to F.S. Nariman, 'the President under the Constitution, has to act and does act in accordance with the aid and advice tendered to him by the Council of Ministers with the Prime Minister as its head. There is no occasion for the President to act in his personal capacity or without reference to the Council of Ministers. Similar views were expressed by Ram Jethmalani who is on record to say that the President is bound to act on the advice of the Prime Minister to dissolve the House.

(*Hindustan Times*, 7.4.1997)

Raghubir Malhotra, a jurist and a constitutional expert is of the view that a National Government is the only way to overcome the present political crisis.

Views of Some Political Leaders

Atal Bihari Vajpayee, BJP leader said, "the ministerpretation of the mandate for the 11th Lok Sabha to anti-BJPism is culminated in the present crisis. At the same time he exhorted all the parties to ponder over why the coalition governments were unsuccessful in the country. (Hindu, 12.4.1997)

According to Ajit Singh, (Bhartiya Kisan Kamgar Party) a coalition government consisting of UF and the Congress would be more suitable at the centre than a UF Government supported by Congress from outside.

Surjit Singh Barnala, the Akali Dal Leader suggested that "the National Government" with representatives from all political formation and an agreed minimum programme was the best way out of the present political impasse. It could also give the country a stable government for the next four years. (Hindu 15.4.1997)

Vasant Sathe, a veteran congress leader also is of the considered opinion that national government is the only answer under the present situation

Speaking to Indian Express (12.4.1997) former President, R. Venkataraman said, "his successor, Shankar Dayal Sharma, should first invite the BJP to form the government once again. The fact that the BJP failed to acquire a parliamentary majority 10 months ago is irrelevant. Whenever a vacancy arises the President has to go strictly on the basis of strength in the Lok Sabha. He must be guided by numbers alone, and leave the rest to the Parliament. Otherwise the office of the President will become a subject of controversy. He said that, in the present situation, the President must explore situation, means to form a government. The dissolution of the Lok Sabha may be envisaged "only after all avenues fail. He recalled that following Chandra Shekhar's resignation in 1991, he had not based the dissolution of the Lok Sabha solely on his recommendation but on the fact that no other political party had come forward to form the government.

Comparing the present situation to that in 1991, when Chandra Shekhar had resigned before the Finance Bill was passed, he said," I had decided not to dissolve Lok Sabha until the budgetary measures were passed by both Houses."

Following is the history of earlier governments when the country was faced with similar situation.

1969: Indira Gandhi lost majority after the Congress split. But she continued to remain in power with the support of the communist parties. Two years later, her recommendation to dissolve the House and go for mid-term polls was accepted by the President.

1979: Janata Party's Morarji Desai lost the vote of confidence. Heading the break away group, Charan Singh staked claim to form the government with the outside support of the Congress. After the Congress withdrew support Charan Singh recommended dissolution of the Lok Sabha and fresh elections. His advice was accepted by President Neelam Sanjiva Reddy.

1991: Prime Minister V.P. Singh and his National Front was reduced to a minority when the BJP withdrew support. Chandra Shekhar's break away group formed the government with the support of the Congress. Later President Venkataraman accepted

Chandra Shekhar's advice to dissolve the House and called for fresh polls. (*Indian Express*, 11.4.1997)

President Venkataraman clarifies now that he did not dissolve the Parliament on the advice of Chandra Shekhar, but dissolved it only after no other party staked their claim.

The situation today is very delicate, there are a good numberof 'aaya rams, and gaya rams', the newly elected members are scared of going to the people again; the political parties are looking to their own interest in comparison to the interest of the people, and the country is practically without any government. There is a complete impasse and a constitutional crisis until the President of India comes out wiih a solution to give this country a stable government.

We reproduce below a relevant portion from H.M. Seervai's book, Constitutional Law of India (An Epilogue, at pages 2718-2719, vol. II), which might help the President to solve the present impasse. It will, of course, serve as a useful guide for all times to come.

On the appointment of Morarji Desai and Charan Singh as P.M. after the fall of Desai's government, the Constitutional expert, Seervai thus explains:

"The President can appoint the nominees of his choice to rule the country for four or five months without ever having had the confidence of the House. The correct course, and the one sanctioned by Art. 75(1) and (3), and by democratic principles, is not to appoint anyone as Prime Minister, if he did not have the support of the majority of the House, dissolve the Parliament, order a general election and let the Ministry which had enjoyed the confidence of the House before it resigned continue to remain in office till the election results were announced. Further to have given Charan singh three weeks' time to secure the support of a majority of the House, and not to have given Mr. Desai the same amount of time can be described as hostile discrimination, the more so as it was the duty of the President to hold the scales even between the two constituents. . . .

As far as can be judged from the published accounts, there is no evidence that the president realised that it was not enough that this or that person could form a Ministry commanding a temporary majority....If the President wanted to scrutinize the claims of support made by Mr. Desai and Mr. Charan Singh, then it was not enough for the President to get the names of the people or parties who said that they supported one or other of the two leaders. It was necessary for the President to obtain in writing that those persons would give general support to one or the other leader for a reasonable period of time to carry on the Government. Had he obtained such writing and the persons failed to act according to their written promise, the President would have been absolved from blame, and the public in the first instance, and the electors in the last, would have dealt with those who had broken their promise.

When Mr. Charan Singh resigned, and the retiring Ministry gave it as their advice that the President should dissolve the House of the People, thereafter the President carried on discussion for a number of days. His discussion was not limited to a simple question whether in law he was bound to follow the advice of the Ministry. It is obvious that he proceeded on the footing that he was not so bound, for, otherwise, he would not have carried on discussions with Mr. Jagjivan Ram who made a claim that he was in a position to form an alternative government and to keep Mr. Jagjivan Ram under the impression that the President would consider the list of members which might be sent to him by Mr. Jagjivan Ram.

In any event, if the object of the President and of all the parties upto that time was to avoid a mid-term poll, it was wrong for the President not to have called upon Mr. Jagjivan Ram to from an alternative government. The fact that the other parties to serve their own interest expressed themselves in favour of a mid term poll, when nothing had changed except that the leader of the largest party expressed his readiness and ability to form a stable government could not absolve the President from his duty to put the interest of the country above the interest of a large number of fragmented and hostile parties. It has been suggested that for the President to have called upon Mr. Jagjivan Ram as the Leader of the Party of 205 Janata M.P.s would have been to encourage defection.

The suggestion can only be described as grotesque after President Reddy called upon the great defector, Mr. Charan Singh, to form a government. As stated earlier, it is much easier for a party of 205 members to secure the necessary support in a House of 544 members than for a leader of about 75 members. It is submitted that the President's action was not only improper and discriminatory, but led to a situation in which he should never have placed the country. He set up a government which never commanded the confidence of the House of the people at all; that government was to remain in power for a period of about 4 months. The President of India has thus presented to the world the humiliating spectacle of a great democratic country being ruled by a Government which never commanded the confidence of the House of the People."

With all humility I repeat, what the former President, R. Venkataraman said in his book "My Presidential Years" on the fall of Chandra Shekhar's Government:

"I did not accept the resignation without feeling sorry for Chandra Shekhar...The office hungry coterie of the Congress Party used to misguide Rajiv Gandhi that Chandra Shekhar's attempts at building up a good image could prove deliterious to his image.

Looking back after two years, I realise my naiveness in accepting Congress Assurance of unconditional support to last a year atleast. I realised that unequal combinations are always disadvantageous to the weaker side."

Over to Rashtrapati ji, and the People of the Country

